The Renaissance of
Motherhood

The Renaissance of Motherhood

By

Ellen Key

Source Book Press

The Renaissance of Motherhood

By

Ellen Key

Author of "Love and Marriage," "The Century of the Child," etc.

Translated from the Swedish by

Anna E. B. Fries

G. P. Putnam's Sons
New York and London
The Knickerbocker Press
1914

The Knickerbocker Press, New York

To

HAVELOCK ELLIS

IN PROFOUND ADMIRATION
AND GRATITUDE

PREFACE

IN this book I have spoken of the social means possible for calling forth a renaissance of motherhood. I have proposed the study of eugenics; a year of social service as preparation for motherhood; state pensions for mothers—which does not imply that the fathers are to be freed from the responsibility.

But the real renaissance must come through the education of the feelings. Many women now advance as the ideal of the future, the self-supporting wife working out of the home and leaving the care and education of the children to "born" educators. This ideal is the death of home-life and family life. No renaissance of motherhood is possible before mothers and teachers, through their own attitude towards the values involved, as through the fiction they give the girls to read, through their own counsels and their scientific sexual enlightenment, prepare the girls' hearts for love and motherhood.   Then young women will again be alive to the truth, spoken by the greatest woman poet the world ever saw:

> " Passioned to exalt
> The artist's instinct in me at the cost
> Of putting down the woman's, I forgot
> No perfect artist is developed here
> From any imperfect woman.   Flower from root,
> And spiritual from natural, grade by grade
> In all our life."
>
> *Aurora Leigh.*

And then will come indeed, the new religion of the new century, the century of the child, now only a hope in the soul of some dreamers.

ELLEN KEY.

STRAND, ALVASTRA,
February 28, 1914.

I

Women and Morals

IT is for women to discover what might be called experimental morality and for us to reduce it to a system. Woman has greater intuition and man greater genius; woman observes and man reasons; and from this collaboration we get the clearest light and the most complete science of which the human mind is capable; in other words, the surest knowledge of one's self and of others which it is possible for humanity to have.[1]

With these words Rousseau expresses an ever living truth, a truth which all great women have confirmed. They have done so through their works as well as through their expressions of opinions about their own sex. Women's strength in all departments—and

[1] "C'est aux femmes à trouver pour ainsi dire la moral expérimental, à nous à la reduire en système. La femme a plus d'esprit et l'homme plus de génie; la femme observe et l'homme raisonne; de ce concours result la lumière la plus claire et la science la plus complète que puisse acquerir de lui-même l'esprit humain; la plus sûre connaissance en un mot de soi et des autres qui soit à la portée de notre espèce."—JEAN JACQUES ROUSSEAU.

that of morals is no exception—has not been of the quality belonging to directly creative genius. Their contribution to the development of morals has grown out of their intuition in regard to the ideal; their swift valuations in the province of experience; their sure eye for the shades rather than the main lines in ethics—quick sympathy in individual cases rather than discernment of fundamental principles.

In the essay which follows, the word "morals" is used to signify the funds of experience which humanity has gained, through pain and joy, and of the actions which possess a life-preserving and life-enhancing value, for individuals as for society. That which benefits body and soul has become good; the opposite, evil. The development of morals consists in an ever clearer understanding of the most active means towards the realisation of the aim just mentioned—pursuing and ennobling the ideal for quickening the intensity of life.

During this process of development (if we except the modern Theosophic and Christian Science movements), women have not served morals as founders of religions; neither have they formed systems of the philosophy of ethics. And had they been given opportunity as lawmakers, they probably would not have created the great works of law. On the other hand, when it comes to the application to life of existing laws and morals, woman, because of her willing receptiveness, her elasticity and adaptability combined with her power of tenacious retention, has exerted an influence, the value of which is too vast to be measured. Neither can its history be written, for it would take the form of countless histories from the animals' lair and the cave-dwellers' hearth to our day, when the mother, happy over some noble deed, strokes the hair from her son's brow, to print the kiss of her approval there; or when with gentle words of wisdom she draws for him the picture of those high possibilities he may be wasting. Or it would picture the wife who, when her husband is called upon to choose between selfish advantage or a higher aim, urges him to sacrifice the advantage to follow his conscience. Or when, from the beginning of history up to our day, women, struggling single-handed, like Antigone of old, have illumined as by a lightning flash the prejudices and baseness that enslaved their age. Or again when, here and there, groups of women have stood side by side with men in willing martyrdom for religion and country, justice and freedom. Or —as in these latter days—when women, at first one by one, afterwards in battalions, fight for their right to equality with men, combining their determination to have their rights with the moral duty actively to fight against all the sin and suffering in which society as yet is buried.

Against these positive contributions by women toward the growth of morals, stand their negative influences: directly through their own actions and indirectly through their encouragement and acceptance of men's non-morality in private and public life. Thus women have sometimes retarded the ethical evolution, sometimes led it astray. To give one example among many: I may remind the reader of the testimonies the Icelandic legends bear to this influence from the day when the men began to allow manslaughter in a family feud to be redeemed with fines, while the women, with tears or scorn, pricked them on to carry out the commands of blood revenge. Or of how, in our day, during the Boer War the majority of English women approved of their own country. Every impartial retrospective survey of the development of morals will show us that just as there have been times when men and women have risen together, there have been times when they have sunk together. It will show us that there have been women who have exercised not merely all the virtues which we justly call womanly, but also those which rightly are called manly. Likewise it will show that women have practised all the vices called masculine, without desisting from those considered especially feminine.

Every generalisation in regard to women and morals of a certain age or country becomes misleading, unless the many exceptions are constantly kept in mind. One such misleading generalisation is, for example, that men have created the code of laws, women the code of conventions,—that is, the unwritten laws which often bind more than the written ones. We need only remember in this connection man's conception of "debts of honour" —for instance, gambling debts—as compared with his ignoring of the debt to the woman he has betrayed; or think how sensitive his honour when prompting to duels, how lacking in regard to the illegitimate children he has brought into life. Such conceptions as knightly honour or warrior pride, business integrity or artistic conscience, indicate a few of those unwritten laws which proffer sufficient evidence that man in his sphere, to a greater extent perhaps than woman in hers, has been a maker of conventions, objectionable and otherwise. It is in the province of home and society that woman has fashioned the customs. Here women's approval and disapproval, wishes and wants, have been quite as formative and reformative as the action of the sea on the mainland. Both in regard to what we ought to do and what we should refrain from doing, from table manners to the behaviour that expresses the presence or absence of love, from superficial refinement to large-hearted deference, it is woman who, in home and society, has been the leader. And to the extent, therefore, that outward behaviour reacts upon inner life, woman has shaped and re-shaped our conceptions of right or wrong. Through quick and strong expressions of sympathy or antipathy for certain thoughts or actions, through a light but incessant pressure,

CONTENTS

she has gradually dissolved or rearranged the strata of our ethical ideas; her persistent disapproval has, drop by drop, made a groove in some strong principle; the unceasing waves of her feelings have rounded our sharp-edged moral commandments.

In many cases, then, woman has modified the moral code, and again has conserved it, by virtue of her stubborn tenacity, which is one with her best traits—tenderness, faithfulness, and piety. This conservatism, on the other hand, is the reverse side of what is intellectually the weakest of her characteristics, her aversion to the serious mental labour involved in the examination of new ideas, her disinclination to the impartial quest of truth, her lack of thirst for objective knowledge. These weaknesses, though less flagrant with an advancing culture, have long made of the average woman a fanatical defender of blind prejudices and obsolete moral laws.

Women's ethical conservatism, however, has been of the greatest importance. On the one hand it gives a training in habits which finally become instincts in regard to what is right; on the other, by treasuring moral assets during periods of transition, which otherwise would have been swept away by evolution—when it has taken on the swiftness of spring floods; finally, by remoulding and thus saving certain indispensable moral gains threatened with obliteration by a new philosophy of life.

In George Eliot, we have a great yet a typical example of women's ethical contribution to the development of moral conception. She, who was an affirmed disciple of Comte and Spencer; who had translated Feuerbach's book against Christianity; who lived in a conscience-marriage, because the man she loved had not fulfilled the forms required for a legal divorce, and who was therefore tied to an unfaithful wife,—she became by her works a golden bridge between the old ethics and the new. Or, rather, she found in her new philosophy of life good and valid reasons for supporting time-honoured moral laws. Her works glorify self-sacrifice, virtue, faithfulness, duty. She demonstrates Nietzsche's satirical words as to the lack of consistency of the Englishman who when discarding Christian faith holds closer than ever to Christian morals.

But the altruism of George Eliot, as that of

other non-Christians, has a deeper foundation. This is upon the fact that countless people, before and after Christianity, are Christians by nature, and that the love of humanity has been practised with more consistency by many so-called heathens than by most confessors of the Christian faith. To George Eliot, life held neither beauty nor order unless lived in altruism, in mutual helpfulness, in sacrifice of one's own happiness for that of others. She founded her ethics on Darwin's then accepted theory of heredity, on Spencer's teaching of the influence of contemporaries and environment upon morals, on Comte's altruistic ethics and his religious intuition of the oneness of humanity. Because of the relativity of morals, she considered it essential that each generation should live in accordance with the standard ethics of its own time. Only thus could morals, during each age, reach the stability necessary for building farther and higher. She was deeply conscious of the controlling power of the present over the future. Every little concession to temptation becomes disastrous by its consequences not only to the individual but also to coming generations. The recognition of this solidarity is more fraught with responsibility than in the case of Christianity. Christianity believes in the forgiveness and expunction of sins. But the new morality is assured of the continuous and uncontrollable consequences of evil as well as of good actions; consequences which persist in wider and wider rings and thus become determining factors for my progeny, my age, my race, aye, the whole of humanity.

"Also deeds are our children, a fruitful and immortal progeny"—George Eliot, who said these words, has crystallised the new thoughts into art in her foremost books where, with true psychological insight, she tells of the fall or victory, perdition or salvation of the soul. She reveals the norm of the ethical life of countless women when she glorifies obedience to the law of human love while at the same time not in a single case does she testify to any value in the individual's rebellion as a means of procuring a higher morality. Tradition, piety, solidarity call forth her admiration. And perhaps she felt a conscious need to emphasise these virtues in order that her own life should not be wrongly followed as an example. Like her great Swedish counterpart

Selma Lagerlöf, she possessed so true a womanly tenderness in her attitude toward men and women that she discovered a treasure-field of redeeming qualities in a fallen soul; aye, she had a Christlike faith in the power of good to overcome evil.

Thirty or forty years ago George Eliot was an unlimited ethical power. She helped all of us who had passed from Christianity to a new outlook on life. She gave us strength in self-sacrifice and comfort in suffering by assuring us that nothing we had suffered would matter a hundred years hence; that the only thing that does matter is what we suffered for. However severe was the education which she offered us to fit us for our responsibilities toward humanity, we all accepted this training with burning gratitude—not the least those of us who learned from her a sense of sober responsibility for that new ethics which she herself did not embrace:—the right of a great love when it proves itself a power to elevate the life of the individual or of the race; the right of personal freedom of choice when the choice blazes a glorious path to new heights; the right of self-assertion in cases where it brings about greater values for the present and for the future than would self-denial; the right of hard-heartedness when my self-sacrifice would harm those for whom I sacrificed myself; and lastly, *the right of the future*. If the past held all the rights to our sacrifices there would be no possibility of developing a higher morality, but only of spreading the established morality over wider areas. Notwithstanding George Eliot and other noble teachers of altruism, as, for instance, Tolstoy, it is, and must ever be, an illusion that altruism is in every case the higher virtue, while egoism is always and in every case on a lower moral plane. Self-preservation and self-development are basic conditions for the practice of altruism. They are duties toward the whole of society as well as to the individual because the elevation of the whole depends upon the highest enhancement of life which each individual attains.

A day's reflection should suffice to make us recognise this truth. On the other hand a whole lifetime will not teach us *how* in each individual case we are to draw the often hair-splitting line between legitimate and illegitimate self-assertion. Self-assertion is illegitimate when it is without value for the whole. Therefore, if either side must be over-emphasised it is important that women in their ethical evolution and in the function of their ideals have shown themselves inclined to assert the power of human nature, especially woman's human nature, on behalf of altruism and sympathy. The noblest women in life or literature have been those who have reached the peace and harmony which are possible only when an ethical norm is realised in their lives. And as this harmony is more readily attained when the norm has been long established and observed, it is but natural that the old-fashioned women as yet offer the loveliest picture, ethically as well as æsthetically. To these women, in our day as in all earlier days, the duty of self-sacrifice has become happiness. They have had the sanction of their conscience as well as the outer sanction of the patriarchal family right, and of the Christian religion. From such conflicts between private and public duties as man's conscience so often encounters, woman has generally been spared. If—for instance in a period of religious transition—she has had to make a choice, it has only meant the exchange of one authority for another. Even when a woman has rebelled within herself against the patriarchal family right, this rebellion only reached her mind, not her conscience, for "conscience is born in the recognition of the difference between ideal and reality." But women's power of moulding ethical ideals was checked by authoritative religion as well as by the conventions which their very ideals supported. Especially was it restrained by the consciousness of the joy women alone possessed: the belief that motherhood, which implied the highest happiness, also enjoyed the *fullest sanction as a duty.* In other words, women's foremost ethical task was not involved in that progress which in other departments of life called for new ethical needs, new aims, new efforts. The home was a closed sphere touched only at its edge by the world's evolution. To protect the young and tend the old within this sphere; to cherish and comfort, guide and restore, train and love, to give pleasure and to help, remained indisputably right during all the world's changes in the domain of home government, of religion, or of economy. Thus in women's life theoretical and practical morals became identical, or, in other words, what from all points of view was objectively right, was also subjectively binding upon her.

With most people the ethical imperative, "You ought," is of little value, while throughout centuries, superstition and fear have at least had a restraining influence. In every age there have been only a small number of true Christians who have lived according to the commandments of Christianity because they loved God. With the rest, fear of the punishment of society and of the torture of Hell has been the restraining force; hope of society's praise and heavenly reward the incentive power. Thus a principle primarily non-moral, yet one which has proved serviceable, in the education of humanity and in the upbringing of children, may by evolution become moral. Objective morals seldom brought in their train other conflicts than those between obedience and disobedience. And, knowing that their own thought and feelings did not suffice to answer the important questions of right and wrong, women enjoyed the effort-saving security of mind belonging to a life led in accordance with the Church's interpretation of the will of God in his Ten Commandments. If this morality of women had not become established through the practice of numberless generations, its splendid manifestation to-day in countless mothers, who, after the day's hard labour, yet have will and strength to promote order, morals, and pleasure in their homes, would be inconceivable.

We have now briefly sketched the pacific relations between woman and morals. The strong democratic movement born in the English Civil War and the French Revolution, which took hold of individuals and commonwealths, included the emancipation of women. This struggle and the struggles which have followed it have produced much moral confusion, but confusion is feared only by him who knows not that evolution awakens needs and desires which in their turn become motive forces toward higher conditions than those long honoured and accepted. Such gains are never made without loss of some old good. Lamentations over the new times are justified only when it can be proved that a better organised or richer life did not evolve from the confusion.

In a retrospect of the transition period we shall often rediscover, in the new gains, values which we had thought lost for ever, but which had only changed their form. Ever since the idea of the emancipation of woman came upon the world's stage, women have begun, consciously and directly, to share in the transformation of existing morals and to demand a new morality, particularly in regard to the relations between the sexes. A century has now seen women labour with ever-increasing energy for the renovation of sex morals. At the same time their new position as self-supporters has indirectly transformed many ethical conceptions and social customs.

Therefore, when we speak of women and morals, we must divide the subject into two parts: the pre-emancipation and the post-emancipation morals,—the morality which originated from the fact that woman was the property of father, husband, and family, and the morality which arose and is yet evolving because this condition is being gradually, if it is not yet entirely, abolished.

All scientific theories of the origin and development of morals, however they may otherwise vary, agree on this one point: that the family is the root out of which—irrespective of differences in religious and social laws—sympathetic feelings have grown and branched

in all directions. Through the child the
family became more than the union of a
man and a woman for the sake of self-pro-
tection. Preservation of the race involves
demands which even in animal life produce
ethical effects of an altruistic character. The
closer the union for common purposes the
more manifold become the ideas of "right"
in regard to married life as well as to the
larger life of society.

What the strong found serviceable became
a duty for the weak. But beside this morality
of expedience, there was at work an influence
of idealistic tendency, whose organ at this
stage was religion. Men judged the earthly
and heavenly goals presented by religion as the
highest, even when they had no tangible association with merit or demerit. However,
the morality which sprang, not from religion,
but from life itself and its needs, remained
the most active of all influence. The affirma-
tions of the religious code of morals became
practical incentives of essential importance
only when they adapted themselves to the new
forms which social life acquired in the course
of evolution.

The necessities of family life naturally resulted in the division of labour which made it man's duty to defend and support the family and woman's to care for the new lives. This division of labour developed in man the so-called manly virtues, in woman likewise the so-called womanly virtues. The former implied more directly what we now call duty toward ourselves, the latter more directly duty toward others. The lower the point at which morality stands, the greater is the gulf between these two spheres of duty.

The history of morals is pre-eminently the history of humanity's endeavour to combine these two spheres of duty by merging into a single ethical system two equally indispensable and valuable fundamental needs, *egoism* and *altruism*. This fusion has taken place both within individuals and within each sex. From certain points of view the weaker sex, so-called, has travelled an easier path than the stronger sex, to developed morality. The fear of the serious consequences which the stronger brought to bear upon the weaker, when the latter had done "wrong," that is, acted to the master's disadvantage, the approval which rewarded "right," that is, action to the master's advantage, has very likely developed women's "sense of duty" more swiftly, and made them more obedient to existing laws and more stubborn in retaining them. Experience, education, example, heredity, laws, and religion combined, however, in the case of both sexes to give stability to morals and acquiescence in the observance of moral laws. When experience, new economic conditions, and new religious doctrines altered men's conceptions of beneficial or harmful conduct ("right" or "wrong") women had to change their ideas accordingly. Their habit of obedience now helped them to overcome the adherence to old customs which the selfsame obedience had created.

In the age of cannibalism, woman considered it "right" to be foodstuff; in savagery, to be a beast of burden; in barbarism, to be a slave. Step by step, the treatment of women, as well as that of the outlawed male prisoners of war, was changed. In both cases, the change took place in consequence of the owner's new ideas as to the most profitable use of his possession.

The conception of sex provided the world with an explanation of its earliest history; in other words, sexual cleavage was considered the cause of the origin and persistence of the world. But although the female principle was worshipped in its divine form—a circumstance which was bound to influence indirectly the estimation of woman—she remained in law and in life on a par with domestic animals, well or ill treated as they. According to the property conceptions of primitive times, wives and children, slaves and stock, were man's possession, to be used by him as he pleased. He might sell, maltreat, or kill them. It hardly needs to be pointed out to what an extent such a view must have retarded the development of man's altruism, while it over-developed woman's obedience. On the other hand, it ought to be stated that among many ancient peoples, as for instance the Egyptians and Babylonians, women possessed rights, in social as well as in private life, which women of our age are still struggling to win. Even in Rome under the Emperors women boasted an economic, social, and domestic equality with men far surpassing what they enjoy in most European nations of the present day.

Marriage was brought about first through spoil, then by purchase, finally through gift.

From the property-right in the wife, thus invested in man, rose the idea that unfaithfulness was a theft from the latter which he arbitrarily punished with death. This conception of unfaithfulness as theft appears plainly from the fact that the man was at liberty to sell or lend his wife to other men. Hence, it was not the sharing of the wife with others which outraged the husband but that this sharing took place without any benefit to him. Women also had to submit when supernumerary or weak children were killed by the father or when he commanded the mother herself to take their lives. With some savage tribes the "duty" of child murder has been a moral law against which woman could not rebel without incurring penalty, or, at least, the contempt of all "respectable" persons.

In no instance is it more clearly shown how morality, at this stage, was bound up with advantage than in this yielding of race-preservation to self-preservation when the latter demanded the death of the offspring either after or before its birth. These once "sacred" duties gradually ceased to exist, partly because of easier conditions of life, but assuredly also because of the will toward the ideal which exists in human nature. For morality in its noblest forms remains inexplicable unless one takes into account that power of growth in the human soul which has led generation after generation from lower religious and ethical standards to higher ones which often clash with worldly advantages. This conflict has caused the majority to advocate the morality of expedience in opposition to the new ethics. On the other hand, however, every now and then some particular example has given impetus to idealism; again it is some rare soul, who from his higher plane has found the customs and laws, supported by the majority, utterly beneath his dignity, that has given that impetus. Obviously the growing motherliness of women has exerted its idealistic and elevating influence on morality with reference to the above-mentioned slaughter of children. Similarly must the wifely faithfulness, in individual women, have sprung from a tenderer feeling for the child's father. But as a rule the chastity of woman has not originated in "woman's nature," but in the mortal fear which adultery brought in its trail. That this has in general been the true state of affairs is best proved by those savage peoples whose unmarried women live loosely, while the wives remain faithful to their husbands. Moreover, married as well as unmarried women have lacked all continence when men have not exacted it of them.

The sphere, on the other hand, where woman's ethics have developed naturally, that is, without external pressure, is motherliness; here the helplessness and loveliness of the child have awakened the instincts of natural sympathy. Tenderness has created the first "social order"—that of the mother with her offspring. Through motherliness woman later makes her great contributions to civilisation.

These contributions are more humane customs and increasingly sympathetic feelings, which gradually are transplanted to the father from the mother. At this stage man's proprietorship in wife and children contributed to a great forward step in his ethical development in that it awoke in him a desire to protect those dependent on him. Neither among ancient peoples nor present-day savages has woman been as barbarously treated as has been commonly supposed. Just as customs in civilised countries give to woman quite a different position from that which the law would indicate, so is it also the case in uncivilised lands.

That woman carries the pack, for example, is due, as E. Westermarck has shown, to the necessity for the man to be instantly prepared for armed battle. In this, as in many other cases, "egoism" has a deeper basis than the seeming one.

Because of her motherhood, woman's sexual nature gradually became purer than man's. The child became more and more the centre of her thoughts and her deeds. Thus the strength of her erotic instincts diminished. The tenderness awakened in her by her children also benefited the father. Out of this tenderness—as also out of admiration for the manly qualities which the father developed in the defence of herself and her children— gradually arose the erotic feeling directed to this man alone. Thus love began. For ages it could not reach a higher form, as woman had no freedom of choice. First in our day and among the highest civilised nations has woman become a free agent in the sight of the law in choosing her life partner. Even among many of these nations, however, the marriage union still bears traces of the earlier times when woman and child were man's property. It is these traces which, for the sake of man's as well as woman's ethical ennoblement, we now desire to eradicate.

In marriage there must finally be perfect equality between husband and wife, in personal freedom of action, in right to earnings and other property, in authority over the children.

For centuries, the forces have been at work which gradually have changed marriage conditions for the better. But in the last century alone, woman has led *directly* in the great battle for higher marriage ethics. Before, she had contributed indirectly to the elevation of such morality. Through the demonstration of their worth, in the first place, but also through the influence of their opinions, mother and wife, daughter and sister, have remoulded man's appreciation of woman; have refined his love and enhanced his sense of justice. Thus the moral transformations already apparent in laws and customs have after all emanated from woman.

The influence of Christianity has been active

at the same time and to a certain extent. But modern moral philosophers, as for instance the already mentioned Prof. Edward Westermarck, contend that this influence has been overrated. Christianity's new outlook on moral values did assuredly exercise a strong *indirect* influence. On the whole it may be said that heathendom glorified the masculine virtues while Christianity glorifies the feminine virtues. Especially may the latter be observed in the cult of the Madonna, which brought about a greater reverence for woman, particularly for the mother. But what the Church gave with one hand it took back with the other. The ancient world looked on marriage as a duty to race and society. The Pauline Christianity permits it, but as a necessary recourse against temptations.

Like other Asiatic religions, Christianity considered sexual life as impure; true purity was attained only in celibacy. When, thus, even the marriage sanctified by the Church was looked upon as a lower state, it stands to reason that when woman, *outside* of marriage, tempted man to unchastity, she was looked upon, to use the strong expression of an Apostolic Father, as the " gate of the Devil."

Every sexual relation outside of marriage was condemned. Thus, if already during heathendom woman's virtue had been judged by her sexual morality, this became the case to still greater degree during Christianity. A woman's "virtue" meant her virginity before marriage and her faithfulness afterwards. As long as death, the pillory, and the whipping-post were the penalties for women's digressions from the path of virtue it was a mother's obvious desire to train her daughter strictly to follow this path. Upon the loss of the daughter's "honour," the fathers vented their curse and society its scorn; while the son's "honour" consisted solely in general human or manly and patriotic qualities.

To be sure, woman's transgressions against life, property, and character were punished in the same way as were man's, and her strength and courage were similarly appreciated. But she was seldom obliged to exercise these virtues or to resort to crime for the sake of economic and juridical self-preservation, as she stood under the protection of the man. Thus man's virtue consisted in courage, energy, pride, honour, and business ability, while his sexual morality was in nowise connected with his "honour" and "virtue." In certain cases, however, for example, abduction, rape, incest, bigamy, and child-murder, the Church demanded self-control even of the man. And certainly the Church contributed greatly to the elevating of sexual ethics in taking a stand for monogamy. But many of these regulations had existed before Christianity, and monogamy was already generally practised in the Roman Empire.

The benefit which ethical development derived from Christianity through a stricter marriage law is counteracted by the heavy debt of the Church to illegitimate children, and to the unhappily married couples held in yoke together in obedience to the commandments of the Church.

In determining the influence of the Church upon sexual morality, account must be taken not only of the sacrifice of the innocent just referred to, but also of the complete falsification of sex morals which grew out of the ecclesiastical point of view. Sexual slavery in matrimony, never discountenanced by the Church, intensified in woman all the vices which man later called "woman's nature." She gained all the blessings of life—motherhood, housewifely honour, support, protection, and enjoyment—if she pleased a man to such an extent that he wanted to marry her. Thus her thoughts, feelings, and actions were all bent in one direction—to please. First in the parental home, then in the home of her husband, woman's prospect of attaining her ends depended upon her ability in shamming obedience and fibbing assent. How then was it possible for the average woman to escape from becoming fawning, flattering, sly, and hypocritical? A self-control forced by outer pressure may, indeed, create good habits, but may equally well result in simulated habits, that is, in falseness. Woman became a coward, because she was not allowed to act on her own risk or responsibility, for, if she made the attempt, she was rudely pressed back into submission.

To what extent all these "woman's vices" will disappear, when the era of woman's full freedom is established, only the future can determine. But already the present age gives fair promise that the slanderers of "woman's nature" will be found in the wrong. The tendencies, considered especially feminine, to self-indulgence, luxury, gossip, and scandal

are neither womanly nor manly. They spring
in either sex from a low ethical and intellectual
culture. And as women, for centuries, have
stood on a lower plane of culture than men of
the same class, women more often have possessed these faults. But they are showing
happy tendencies to diminishing proportions,
the more woman's culture advances. Constantly increasing numbers of women are
learning, through scientific studies, for instance,
subjection to truth, intellectual probity, unselfish perseverance. And this new ethic
must also work a change in their private lives.

In the measure that the rich women are
released from the housewifely labour through
new industrial conditions of production, they
become idle and incapable. Countless are the
women parasites who, to satisfy their craving
for pleasure and luxury, impoverish father or
husband. These lame limbs in the social
organism, which themselves accomplish nothing, but for whom all other limbs work, are
the most flagrant example of womanly immorality in the present. And they live in
this immorality without a trace of compunc-
tion. As a result of this parasitism, erotic
interest has become the whole content of life

to these women. Under the influences of many centuries of sex-slavery, the erotic life has developed at the expense of other sides of woman's nature. And our age unfortunately still possesses a class of women who as sex beings only desire sensual gratification. When women have reached this stage, sex-hatred is near, a hatred which is likely to be the last phase of sex-slavery.

There are no more dangerous enemies in the ethical campaign for the liberation of women than this class which drags sexual morality down to the animal plane.

II

If, as some men contend, the above-mentioned severe judgments of woman's morality, during the period of sex-slavery, were all there was to say about this morality, we might well hasten from the past and the present to the future. But fortunately, woman's ethics during pre-emancipation have brought humanity immeasurable values. In the first place, motherhood not only developed sympathy and altruism, it also called forth a whole group of virtues which man seldom noted, because to him they seemed just as naturally to belong to the woman as the milk which flowed from the mother-breast to the lips of the child. Kant's definition of virtue as that which is difficult, that which breeds apathy and demands self-mastery, has a long pedigree in the estimation of morals. Because woman's sex virtue was difficult, it perforce became her true "virtue." Her other ethical attainments—patience, considerateness, thriftiness, etc.—were taken for granted, were considered her natural characteristics, as were also her devotion and willingness to sacrifice herself; like the atmosphere, they were only noticed when absent. All the qualities developed in the care of children, as in other early spheres of women's work,—farming, handiwork, etc.,—were no more "natural" than the vices produced by sex-slavery. But the stimulus from without to the virtues mentioned may be traced to self- as well as race-preservation. By reason of the power which associations of ideas wield over feeling, will, and thought, these virtues, which had been produced as it were automatically, were consequently little appreciated, while woman's relation to the sex morality demanded by men settled her ethical worth.

During this one-sided moral training, right, that is the sexual self-mastery which once roused her disinclination because enforced, became gradually her inclination, or in a more beautiful word, her happiness. She realised that man's demand that the children he supported should be his own helped to inspire his love for them, and that thus her faithfulness to him contributed to their welfare. She realised that legalised motherhood gave the children the devotion and protection of their father, while illegal motherhood deprived them of those blessings. She realised that she could give the children better care because of the protection marriage afforded. Faithfulness then became a demand, dictated not by superficial life alone but by its inner reality, and a demand which won her personal approval.

That the mother grew into closer relationship with the child was a natural consequence of her greater physical and psychical contribution to it. This deeper feeling of the mother for the child was, and is, consciously and unconsciously, the innermost reason why chastity finally has become with many women a second nature, which consequently costs them no struggle and needs no coercion. The feelings of sympathy and consideration produced by family-life and housemother duties scattered women's emotions in several directions, and in the degree to which they grew cooler erotically the more sensitive did they become in reference to their sexual integrity, and especially did they guard this integrity when they themselves loved.

Thus out of the animal sex instinct there gradually evolved human love—that is the dedication of soul and senses to one individual to the exclusion of all others. In love of the husband, as earlier in love of the child, were focussed all the noblest virtues of woman, her most sublime self-sacrifice. Just as this love of husband and wife also led her to criminal deeds when her general moral level was lower than that of her love. Hence, when, in any ethical department, unity is attained between outer demands and inner desires, between nature and conscience, between the needs of society and the individual, the moral formula is void, because inner necessity then makes it psychically and physically impossible to break the outer law. Thus true morality is attained.

From woman's realisation of the fact that her sexual morality was of greater importance to the race than that of man, followed her deliberate or thoughtless acceptance of the double standard which exists even in our day. Men continue to judge women, and the latter to judge themselves and each other, according to sexual relations. Such relationship has determined women's honour or dishonour, morality or immorality, in a mode extremely perilous to their general human morals. The "fallen" woman was not she who lied or belied, hated or intrigued; not she who at home daily behaved in a way which made the home a hell for its inmates. No, not even she who stole, murdered and committed arson; such a woman was only "criminal", not "fallen." "Fallen," once and for ever, was only the woman who outside of marriage allowed herself the natural expression of one side of her life. Fallen is she even if the most soulful love caused her "fall." This estimation of woman's morality has, consciously and unconsciously, lowered man's respect for the woman he has seduced or for the one who has freely given herself to him. His conscience has remained asleep because neither public opinion nor his mistress has awakened it.

Hence the deserted women have been tempted to all the crimes which result from this standard for woman's morality.

It is well known that female criminals— or at least those punished by law—are everywhere far less numerous than male criminals. In Sweden, for example, only one in seventy criminals is a woman; in England, on the other hand, one in five, because there alcohol, the main source of male crime, also attracts women. In connection with woman's lesser criminality we must remember her position, always more protected than man's; her greater fear of consequences, induced by her livelier imagination; but especially must we remember the fact that when the man, unable or unwilling to work, becomes a thief or a white-slaver (according to recently published statistics, Chicago alone had 1500 white and 300 coloured men in this trade), the woman similarly constituted becomes a prostitute. Likewise it is this livelihood which women with starvation wages, unemployed, or just out of prison often resort to, while men in the same predicament choose some expedient which brings them into more immediate conflict with the law.

In judging the murders and thefts committed by women, we must especially take into consideration the influence of the great cities. Here flourish the desire to attract attention, the craving for luxury, all the hysterical desires which, in both sexes, lead to crime, or cause them to entice each other. We know how often a woman is at the root of a man's evil deed, and a man behind the crime of a woman. But the main causes of crime in the large cities are, and ever will be, want, bad housing, and the lack of wholesome joy. That women of the labouring classes do not oftener become criminals under the influence of the atmosphere of the large cities is a high testimony to woman's morality; we know, on the other hand, that the female parasites of luxury in the great cities often turn out to be master-thieves, in never paying their dressmakers and other purveyors.

Nationality must also be taken into account when we consider the crimes of women. As an instance, with the Germanic peoples, respect for life is greater than with the Romanic.

Woman, however, as the bearer and guardian of the new lives, has everywhere greater respect for life than man, who for centuries, as hunter and warrior, learned that the taking of lives may be not only allowed, but honourable. Woman's greater reverence for life probably also contributes to the fact that suicide is comparatively rare among women. Woman's subconscious respect for her own body as the origin of the new race, together with her physical timidity, probably restrains her in regard to this crime, which, moreover, by the Church, for many centuries, was considered the worst of all.

Most crimes committed by the female sex, whether against written or unwritten laws, are in some way connected with the sex morality of the time. Abortion, child-murder, and such crimes are women's special temptations, particularly in countries where society passes its harshest judgments upon unmarried mothers. And these women are certainly not, as a rule, the worst kind. On the contrary, it is often because of love for the child that they commit the crime which but a few days' care of the baby life would have made impossible. Prison chaplains have testified that the infant murderers constitute the moral élite among the prisoners. A striking manifestation of the preposterousness of the present norm for woman's morality!

An indirect consequence of the existing double standard is, that most women's ideas of right and honour in social questions have remained just as dull as most men's conceptions in regard to sexual questions. The easy conscience with which women secretly trespass against the law has often struck man with amazement. He ought instead to wonder that women's social morals are not worse. Those thinkers and writers who have talked of woman's "criminal nature," of her "moral weakness," have never proved anything but that the women from whom they have gathered their experiences have been ill-chosen by themselves. It is still more amazing to find woman—who as citizen, in many important questions, is absolutely without rights—on great occasions in the life of the nation showing herself fully equal to man in a sense of duty and willingness to self-sacrifice. Many mothers, besides the Spartan and the Japanese, have sent their sons to battle for their country; many women have become martyrs for the truth they themselves have embraced. And in our day the working-women within the socialist ranks have developed a sacrificing spirit and a solidarity which prove that the new ethical demands of a progressing world find the same response in women as in men.

But on the whole, the experience that the activity of the soul obeys the law of least resistance has been verified even in regard to women's social morals. As a rule these have been focussed on the family and on charity; among other reasons, because woman's sense of duty seldom finds means of expression in other directions. Man's highest morality, exemplified in his sacrifices for unselfish aims, his fearless search for truth in the fields of thought and faith, his burning desire for justice for all, has only in exceptional cases and in agitated times been achieved by woman. The essential condition for all activity, *opportunity to act*, has been denied to woman, and thus the stimulus of her moral ambition and the development of her social responsibility have necessarily been retarded. To be sure, social morality has demanded even of woman that she take her allotted place in a higher unity, that she, for instance, in times of distress, make sacrifices for her country or her fellows. But in everyday life this higher unity has never been too great to be embraced within her arms. The ethical principle, the greatest possible happiness for the greatest possible number—for whose realisation the struggles of the present age are raging—this principle woman in her little sphere has easily been able to apply. What her conscience has commanded, her heart has affirmed and her reason has harmonised with her will.

It does not necessarily follow that women's feeling of responsibility, even in regard to the home, has been sufficient.

The production of the requisites of the home during the age of domestic manufacture developed in women a great capacity for work which was also well compatible with joy in work. But although woman gradually improved the art of cooking, of dressing, and of other home occupations, we must admit the truth of men's contention on the one hand, that all ingenious creatures within this ancient sphere of woman's labour have been men, and on the other hand that the average level of women's proficiency has been low; and again, that in the departments where the duty and custom of centuries ought to have taught them efficiency, the majority still bungle. This is especially true in the field of education. Not only is there a dearth of creative genius among women educators, but more, the majority of women have not an inkling even of the purport of *true* education. The same may indeed be said of many men who, as a rule, do not accomplish the best possible in their sphere of work. Yet the difference in woman's and man's business pride is just as indisputable as its reason is easily found. Man's work is appraised by customers and employers, while woman's work has been uncontrolled and irresponsible, a field of activity where man's discontent alone could cause an improvement if needed. Woman's want of economic means also combined to make her practical contributions toward improved labour methods of rare occurrence. But the most important reason was, and is, that woman's conservatism found the old customs good enough, and that no one has expected of her a higher insight than the advice inherited from mother and grandmother in regard to the care of children and home.

The economic and moral consequences of woman's lack of experience in handling money are everywhere noticeable. What she ought to purchase for money provided by the husband; how to discriminate between essentials and non-essentials; absolute or temporary needs; when to save or when to spend—all these are conceptions of duty in domestic management yet lacking in women. In these questions of right, women are yet sinning greatly through thoughtlessness and ignorance, shiftlessness and laziness. This is where they ought to *love their neighbour;* that is, the physical and spiritual well-being of those nearest to them. And these sins are not most rare among classes where means are plentiful to provide for the health and comfort of the family.

Women's flippant self-content in the fulfilment of their duties remained with them when they began to enter the field of remunerative labour. Women accustomed to manual labour soon learned through necessity to produce satisfactory work. But women of the upper classes—for instance, widows and daughters who, upon the death or failure of the family supporter, were compelled to earn a livelihood—were in no way prepared for this necessity. When free to choose, their first concern was to find the easiest and most refined work, not that which they could do *well*. They expected the same privileges as the home-worker; for example, indifference on the part of their employers to promptness, freedom to rest unnecessarily, to waste time, never to be ready at the time promised, etc. And especially did the notion prevail that the remunerative labour could be carried on with the same dilettantism as the home work.

Stern necessity has taught women more and more to discard these bad habits, and now they frequently excel men in moral devotion to business. In connection with the demand for professional training as a condition for women's employment, their labour efficiency shows a rapid growth. Wives and daughters from the well-to-do classes, who have never come in contact with the hard conditions of life, because a man has protected, and decided for, them; who have never received the economic ethical education which only personally earned means can bestow; who have never handled any but "pocket money," "gifts" from men,—such women have learned in an amazingly short time to become capable of work, to become economically independent members of society.

Women had grown accustomed even to conceal as "unwomanly" their longing for knowledge, work, and economic independence. During the days of sex-slavery woman learned "instinctively to hide all which she thought might detract from her in men's eyes, even her best qualities when she imagined they might incur man's ridicule or displeasure."[1] Economic necessity has now forced her to become more frank. In a generation, enterprise, venturesomeness, and self-confidence have grown apace with competence. Less and less often do you hear a woman sigh, "I want to so much, but I cannot" or "I may not"; more and more often do you hear her express the words formerly considered "unwomanly," "I want to, and what I want to do I can do."

Among the economic ideas with a moral bearing which it would seem that women might have been able to originate is co-operation. Yet they have failed to take the initiative. Since the movement gained a start, however, women of the present day have

[1] Havelock Ellis.

begun wisely to work together to improve domestic as well as social work. Here they have found new use for the most desirable qualities developed in the best of them from the time of primitive home-production: forethought, thrift, managing ability, and sense of beauty, all virtues which they have intensified by a methodicalness, promptness, and discipline not possessed by their grandmothers.

To what an extent these new women still have retained their devotion and willingness to sacrifice themselves is best shown by the many women, supporters of families, who now work outside of the home for those dependent upon them, with as much tenderness as they formerly worked within the four walls of the home.

It remains for women, whether working in public or private life, to learn another duty, the art of living. To overwork until a nervousness sets in which finally precludes self-control; to throw one's self into social activities to such an extent that the home-life suffers; to allow wrangling, nagging, and fault-finding to mar the family life; to bring pressure and constraint to bear where no ethical values are to be gained; to miss a sense of

4

proportion between labour and rest—all these are shortcomings in the art of living, an art which is sadly undeveloped in modern women as well as in men. The good old phrase "charity begins at home" needs recognition as a serious principle of duty. Perhaps the most immoral consequence of the patriarchal family conception lies in the fact that for ages the family ties have been valued as immutable assets and therefore without apprehension hidden in the bottom of the chest as so much cold gold. One locks it in; it is not supposed to need nursing. Even those who do not fail in the duty of "loving their neighbours" fall short in fulfilling the duty of being lovable at home as abroad.

The art of living demands that our interest in bringing forth flowers in our family life equal the interest we take in bringing them forth in our window gardens. So long as their home-life *æsthetics* have not become *ethics*, women need not expect husbands, children, or servants to feel happy in the homes of their creation. With women as with men, with the old as with the young, with the heads of the household as with the servants, the dying out of the patriarchal customs and the fixed and authoritative philosophy of life have brought in their train a serious levity in the life of the individual, the home, and society. Everywhere subjective inclination is followed in lieu of objective norms. No one need fear but what new principles will gradually crystallise out of all this formlessness, so that the human relationships will again be invested with a new and noble garb. But thus far the self-denial and self-control which made family life beautiful in the past are sadly lacking in the home habits and social customs of the present day. And such traditions are not merely empty shells. They enclose and guard a kernel of ethical value. They are educational means of spiritual and moral import which the modern women utilise neither in their own interest nor in that of their children. The need of a change in this respect is already so deeply felt that we hear everywhere calls for a renaissance of the home and social life.

A more individualised ethical conviction as the sole guide in the *great private decisions* of life; a more and more uniform morality in *public life;* a good tone in social life common to all classes, sexes, and ages,—this is the goal women should set for their contribution to the growth of morals. If women really desire to "save home and society," as they have stated, while demanding new rights, then the road to such salvation lies in a more deliberate guarding of the best in the old conditions combined with all the good gifts of latter-day evolution. Women must, as a moral duty, combat, in themselves and in others, inclination not only to shirk work, but to bustle in work; they must consider as sins all habits which disturb the healthful normal proportions in life. They must favour all tendencies to the saving of the human energies for higher purposes; they must further all kinds of co-operation which purposes to satisfy best and most economically all the needs of the day; and not least the need of rest, and joy in work. The women who stand highest do already exercise these duties, but on the whole, the conception of duty in this respect is confused by the Christian doctrine of self-sacrifice on the one hand and the zeal for social work on the other.

III

Since women have undertaken remunerative labour, outside of the home, an occupation forced upon them by the changed economic conditions, methods of production, and their simultaneous struggles for emancipation, the problems of women's morals have multiplied and women's conceptions of morals have broadened. Out of the demand for the *right to work* grew the realisation of the *duty to work;* from the realisation of this duty, the *honour of labour* was born, and from the honour of labour the step to *social work* was short.

The more women have developed their common human qualities, the more have they been right in their demand that their morality be measured by another measure than that of sex morality, and also that man's sex morals should be considered in the judging of his morality. Thus the modern woman has endeavoured both to widen the sphere of her moral duty and to narrow man's moral liberty.

In other words, woman has had the audacity to apply the principle of individuality even to sex morals and thus to proclaim that neither in man nor in woman should blind obedience to moral traditions, but the verdict of the individual conscience in the first place, and the effect on society in the second place, become the determining factor. The influence on society must without question determine our objective ethics, but such precepts need not always nor everywhere coincide with the subjective moral obligation. The trend of a woman's will, her ethical ideal, must be taken into account when judging her actions as has long been done in the case of man. In the sphere of morality, woman will no longer be content to cultivate the sympathetic feelings and sex virtue. She wants to express her whole self in her life-plan; she will be guided sometimes by altruism, sometimes by egoism, with the right to decide when the one or the other will best subserve her larger life. This has led the modern woman into numberless conflicts between individual and social duty. The pictures Ibsen has drawn of such conflicts have shaken our consciences, but even earlier they have appeared in literature when the latter has been great enough to mirror the whole life of contemporary times.

Some of woman's new moral battles have taken place in the sphere of national life; for example, the Russian women's participation in the political revolution, often in the form of nihilistic attempts on life. We have another example in the English suffragette's mode of warfare. A comparison favours the Russian women, for the reason that they have tried, through their actions, to expose extreme wrongs to *all*, wrongs which would not be known except through deeds of violence. The English women have set out from the wrong notion that because men, driven to political despair, have committed deeds of violence, women also should in cold blood conceive and organise similar outrages. Thus they do *not* act rashly, but with great forethought, driven onward by the delusion that they cannot win the political right to prove how much better a world created by both men and women would be, unless they use the lowest weapons employed by men in this "man-made world."

The enthusiasm and generosity even unto death of the suffragettes are as strong as their social thinking is weak. To commit crime for the sake of gaining the right to benefit society—in other words, to apply the Jesuit maxim, "The end justifies the means"—is ethically so untenable that we can overthrow the fallacy at once with the question, May not these women, following out their mode of thinking, later commit election frauds or other demoralising actions during political campaigns? In America, women have already cheated at elections. And why should they not do so everywhere if they were able thereby to assure the election of the candidate in favour of their noble reform plans? The unconditional no, with which even the suffragists answer this question, stamps the entire suffragette morality as a remainder of the masculine morality in politics, a morality which would stoop to acquire justice and power through violence. To be sure, Spencer's opinion that all violent transformations in the social order are harmful, is historically proved to be an exaggeration. But history has also proved without a doubt that the fruits of a successful revolution are easily lost, for the psychological reason that those who long have lacked rights and then take them by storm, seldom are able to keep them, and are even less able to use them wisely. The social reconstruction we look forward to through woman's suffrage will prove a structure of loose bricks without cement to hold them together, unless a higher morality than man has shown in the past constitute its binding element.

In passing, it should be emphasised that the

very idea of the emancipation of woman has been hitherto one of the greatest stimuli of higher idealism in modern times, and thus a strong force for moral advance. Those who are able to dream have had the most beautiful visions of the woman of the future, just as the socialist in his dreams sees the perfected society of the future. True, neither the future woman nor the coming state will ever reach the beauty of our dreams. But the dream has uplifted the dreamers ethically, and given strength and renewed strength to millions of tired struggling men and women to persevere in the battle without which neither the future woman nor the future state ever will become anything but dreams. But are we to believe that the deeds of the suffragettes, by virtue of the ideal sacrificial spirit which stimulates them, are "the stuff that dreams are made of"? Hardly.

The present-day women, who thus through their sense of justice have become criminals, are fortunately few compared with all those who, with the same burning will to self-sacrifice and with wholly clean weapons, have fought for their sexual rights, and for many common human rights. These latter women ought to have atoned in the eyes of men for their sisters' Jesuit morality.

For more than a hundred years, women—at first always called "unwomanly" and "immoral"—have worked unceasingly for the elevation of social morals. We find them active in movements for better care of the sick and prisoners, in combating alcohol and prostitution, in improving conditions of labour, housing, and general sanitation. They are working for the protection of motherhood and childhood, for the education and healthful recreation of the masses and of children. They share generously in the care of the poor and aged. They are a powerful factor in the question of peace and arbitration. It is not with words alone that they have proved their right to full citizenship; an enormous sum of ethical and altruistic exertions already supports such a claim. And this manifestation of energy has brought about a corresponding improvement in women's social responsibility, an improvement which has reacted favourably also upon men, who, in this department, have not taken as broad initiatives as women. We may well aver that men's and women's ethical views combined have accomplished that awakening of the social conscience which has manifested itself more generally in the last century than before in a thousand years. Social motherliness has made women's struggle for liberty the loveliest synthesis of egoism and altruism.

George Eliot's words already quoted are true also of the modern women: the more they have freed themselves from the authority of ecclesiastical Christianity, the more eager they become to convert the commands of Christian love into social actions. And, fortunately, women's practical sense has prevented them from following the programme of a Tolstoy, which is too incompatible with real life to serve as a foundation for creative social work. Women's contributions to this work have ushered in the "*moral sans sanction ni obligation*" which Guyau preached. A moral founded on the sympathetic instincts, the feeling of solidarity, the spirit of mutual helpfulness, because these categories best promote the well-being of the individual as well. We observe the realisation of Guyau's optimistic assurance: that sympathy, love, and pity more and more become, not only a matter of conscience, but a source of happiness.

Social motherliness, unfortunately, has its hands still bound in countless cases where they are most needed. And if ever a right has been demanded from altruistic motives, it is true in the case of woman suffrage and the married woman's right over self and property.

IV

Women's social morality, like the bean of the Hindu fakir, has thus grown from night to morning to a tall stalk. But we must not forget that the stalk throws a shadow!

As soon as one is not content with a dogmatic simplification of the life problems, the woman morality of our day becomes the most complex of all modern problems. No factor must be left out of account if this is to tally with truth.

And the truth is that the social work, just as much as the remunerative work, has become a natural expression of women's self-assertion and of their desires to utilise all those personal forces to which may be applied the Dutch proverb *rust roest* (rest rusts, or, in rest rust appears). *In the meantime other forces have remained practically unused.* Such opponents to feminism as contend that woman's political influence will debilitate the people's virility, weaken their laws, retard their national self-assertion, are less likely to prove true prophets than those who fear the opposite: that women will become more and more manlike.

Public life has become a strong stimulus, a stimulus no longer found in the home. Ambition has developed into a passion which drives women, as well as men, to great works—and small deeds. Formerly competitors in the race for men, they are now competing in the race for social tasks and distinctions. The social morality of the younger women has improved more than their personal morality, which is the same as that of their mothers and grandmothers. The older generation still sees duty in the direction of overcoming temptations to anger and vengeance, arrogance and vanity, temper and self-deception. The new ethical will of the younger generation is for knowledge, work, and social activity. But all this gives little time for the daily self-examination so necessary for persistent efforts toward ideal goals. Sweden's great saint, Birgitta, took a bitter herb in her mouth, each time she was angry, to chastise her tongue. The woman of the present day has not even time to bite her tongue upon like occasions! All that which formerly belonged to the conception of sanctification and made man introspective, has small place in his present superficial life. Ever fewer present-day men and women find time for the individual culture which makes the soul more serene, gentle, wise, and at the same time broad; which makes the personality harmonious through its emancipation from externals. And yet there is nothing we need more in our strenuous age than moral culture, or, if we prefer so to call it, the morals of culture. Our lack of self-discipline has been given a medical not a moral name; it is called "nervousness" and "hysteria" and is given sanatorium treatment. But this is far from being the only cure needed to restore balance to this age suffering from mental St. Vitus dance. The successes of Christian Science and similar movements depend upon their teaching the duty of continuous self-examination and self-control, that these are made the condition for the dietetics of the soul about which the German physician, Feuchtersleben, long ago wrote a splendid little book. Lately two Danes, L. Fejlberg and C. Lambek, have written excellent books dealing with the greatest possible yield of spiritual forces and, concerning a form of culture of personality as yet unknown to most people. I mean a culture productive of values which cannot be called directly moral because they determine all the conditions of the soul. We may learn an art of living by which the soul can grow in alertness and candour, in mobility and warmth, in height and depth. And this art women should be the first to acquire. If we prefer, we may call it the gymnastics of the soul by which the spiritual "organism" is kept elastic and succulent instead of growing stiff and dry. We may make our feelings warmer, our interests richer, our mental conceptions clearer, our observations broader, our sentiments more serene, our judgments wiser, our will more swiftly steered toward worthy goals. Only by considering *such a culture of the resources of our soul as an ethical duty* can we develop the fulness of personality indicated. The essential requisites for such culture are *psychologic insight, determination, peace,* and *time.* But how is it possible for the ever busy mortals of to-day to take cognisance of all this? Ask an active club member if she has drawn deeply once a year from some well of wisdom in her library; or if Sunday is made a day of rest to body and soul; or if she once a week receives a deep impression from nature or music, or if when seeking such inspiration, she has had the inner repose which allows the impressions to flood the soul, and not only to reach the eye and the ear.

If women's new social morality shall in truth lift humanity not only out of misery, but up to a nobler spiritual affluence, then their own soul culture must attain heights not yet dreamed of by the majority even of our most excellent women to-day. The disheartening evidence of the truth that woman's soul-culture has not developed to the extent that her desire for freedom has grown is found in *the domain of sexual ethics*. First we observe as a sad result of present economic conditions an increasing number of women who, although well fitted to propagate the race, yet involuntarily are doomed to remain dry branches on the tree of life. The consequence is a manifold degeneration even in the sphere of morality, because the never appeased yearning for love and motherhood causes many abnormal situations and mental conditions. Further we find married women losing ability, or will, to become mothers, some on account of overwork, others on account of a frivolous desire for pleasure. Finally we note how in the last hundred years, the severe labour conditions wreck mothers as well as children. It will take another century of unceasing effort to overcome all this psychical and physical degeneracy.

This demoralisation alone shows us plainly enough to what a pass the world, governed exclusively by men, has come.

But besides these facts of a purely statistic nature, which prove that "evolution" is not always synonymous with progress, there are other evidences that do not admit of being stated in figures, which give similar testimony.

George Eliot was the highest representative of womanly conservatism in the sphere of morality. Another woman, George Sand, is the fiery proclaimer of woman's right to freedom, particularly in the same department. She utters one of the few truths which have eternal life, when she calls legal marriage without mutual love immoral, but true love even without legal marriage moral. The consequence of this maxim is that all the remainders of sex-slavery in present-day marriage make it immoral as an *institution* even when the individuals stand higher than the institution. *Only the free giving under perfect equality can make the marriage relationship moral*, that is, found it on an *inner* necessity, not an *external* coercion. But unfortunately George Sand herself showed by the long string of her misadventures that the greatest problem is to find and to keep the *one and true love*. Alas, she became herself an argument against her creed, an argument which may be condensed into the question: Is love always moral? Are many successive unions really of higher value for the life enhancement of the individual and the race than the unbroken or loveless marriage? And even if we answered yes for the individuals themselves there is the next question: Are the children better served by the successive marriages and free unions than by a home where the parents are held together not by love but by a sense of duty toward the children?

At present these questions can only be answered in each separate case.

But in spite of all the confusion and error brought about by the new sex morals, it is nevertheless on these that woman must build further in order to secure for *the future a higher morality*. This good must include the best of what we have gained genetically in the matter of sex morality, namely, *a love invested with a will to faithfulness and continuity*—together with the best of the new morality, namely, the conviction that *chastity consists in the harmony between soul and senses*, and that *no sexual relationship is moral without such harmony*. Women's greatest ethical task is first to combine *these two principles* and then to bring them into *full accord with reality*.

Hitherto women, unfortunately, have not proved themselves competent to this mission. Their instincts are injured, partly by centuries of asceticism and resignation, partly by the present day's violent rebellion against these very limitations. Love, in common with other great powers,—as the demands for freedom, and justice,—is a valuable incentive to ethical action only when dictated by objective as well as subjective morals in harmony with each other. In other words, incentive for actions that directly may promote the richer life of the individual while by their consequences they similarly must benefit the whole. That two persons' love may cause other persons to suffer—just as the demands of justice and liberty often have caused such sufferings—does not prove that any of these feelings in themselves have been illegitimate. When choosing our ethical positions we must not allow these sufferings to become the determining factor. And on the whole they have never had such an effect. Indeed the road of all ethical progress has been marked by the sufferings of individuals, of classes, and of whole nations. The question to be answered is: Will the action which brings pain to others promote an advancing, not a retrogressive, evolution? But this examination has been shirked by many who, in word or deed, have led the struggle against sex-slavery. During this time of sex emancipation, we have come to see that the sex morality beaten into woman was neither so general nor so deep-rooted as one might have expected after all the ages of pressure of law and custom. Very few of the women who have given themselves in free love to a man have had a right to plead the words in which Kant's disciple, Schiller, expressed a great truth:

A man who loves passes so to speak beyond the bounds of all other ordinances and stands beneath the laws of love alone. There is an exalted condition in which many other duties, many other moral standards, are no longer binding upon him.

The feelings that have determined the actions of these women have *not* brought forth "an exalted condition." Their love has never been the great love the essential characteristic of which is its ability to kindle soul and senses, but also, beyond that, to increase the personality's value to life, not only life's value to the personality of the lover. Above all, the great love also kindles that tenderness which is indispensable to lovers. In the great love, desire becomes loathing if the soul remains solitary. With most present-day so-called "soul-mates" the right to happiness has revealed itself as a paltry desire for stimulation in new enjoyments. The demand to "live one's life" has resulted in a more and more vulgar gratification of an ever more inane desire. Not even *The Great Passion* ever grazed these people with its wing; much less did *The Great*

Love ever enter their dreams. Soulless lust, idleness, sentimentality, flights of fancy, vanity, the excitement of flirtation and sport —all of these have been the cause of hasty divorces, loose relations, repeated trial marriages, all distinguished by a greater minus of soul and a steadily growing plus of coarseness. How many wives are there not—and among them even mothers, who in their children possess the richest life stimulus—or how many home girls with splendid life possibilities, who, more or less secretly, lead the life of a courtesan. The only difference is that these women are not paid. On the contrary, they themselves often pay, that is, in form of "loans," which those invertebrates, to whom alcohol, nicotine, silk-linings, and automobiles are necessities of life, do not hesitate to solicit, once these women have become their "comrades." These weaklings often belong to literary and artistic bohemian circles where men have the leisure to win women from the social strata here referred to. These milksops try to make up for their lack of creative genius by all kinds of pleasure sensations, especially the enjoyment of women. Our age has also produced a type of women, the counterpart of these moral mollusks and with the same kind of life cravings equally intense. Add the pristine feminine needs of luxury and pleasure, and you meet a class of modern women of the same variety as the men referred to who use the property of their mistresses for their private ends or coax their earnings from them.

It is not alone man's craving for pleasure that women have made their own, but also the masculine bad manners in outward demeanour. One had hoped that women's companionship with men would check coarseness. And this is true in coeducational schools. But where freer forms for social intercourse prevail, we observe nonchalant and flirtatious young women adopting the manners of their masculine companions. Many young girls resemble noisy, ill-mannered schoolboys. The real reason for this is the womanly fear of displeasing the man friends by so-called "womanishness." But in proportion as the social intercourse between the sexes loses in courteousness and modesty, the erotic life sinks to a lower plane. If the young women want to prevent this, they must raise the standard for men, not lower their own.

Obviously the love which is lacking in will for continuity must also be devoid of the yearning for perpetuity which reaches after the child. Motherhood is avoided or prevented. Sometimes it is the man who for selfish reasons is undesirous of progeny. In such cases, he has himself to blame if the wife in love adventures seeks the life interest which a child would have given her. All this is called the new immorality of our age. But we know very well that it is not *new;* history often shows similar conditions during transitional periods. I would not have touched upon them here were it not that the modern courtesans define their mode of life as the *new morality* instead of owning to its ancient designation: "*unchastity.*" Through this confusion of ideas the lives of many worthy men and women are ruined. And the consequence will not be a new morality, but, on the contrary, a violent reaction back to the old sex morality!

The revision of this old morality among its many other good results has changed our point of view in regard to the "fallen" women, so named even when in true love they became mothers. In the fifties, Mrs. Gaskell in her novel *Ruth*, and Hawthorne in *The Scarlet Letter*, made the first earnest attempts to effect a revision of the judgment over unmarried mothers, a revision which has been going on ever since. The most important new gain in the department of sexual ethics is this very changed attitude toward unmarried mothers, who, together with their children, are now beginning to get the care long refused them by society. But even in this department the humaneness of modern times has been at fault through too much sentimentality and too little forethought. For instance, we call motherhood holy, oblivious of all the miserable human progeny which, married as well as unmarried, mothers cast upon society. A greater severity in the judgment of such mothers must supplement the new conception of the unmarried mothers' status; otherwise, the intrinsically necessary protection of mothers will result in a diminished sense of responsibility. What can be more immoral than to ask the strong and healthy members of society to burden themselves with increasingly heavy taxes in order to support the vicious human offscum, and, moreover, allow this class to propagate its kind? The bygone custom of putting children to death showed a much higher morality from the point of view of *social ethics*. The changed conception of sexual morals has influenced also our attitude toward the woman prostitute. Van Lennep's book *Klaasje Levenster* filled a crying need in that it acquainted "virtuous" women with the fact that there are many innocent victims among the prostitutes. And besides the direct prey of the white slave traffic, there are the indirect victims of the starvation wage still suffered by millions of women. Happily a Dumas, a Tolstoy, and other writers have shown us that great love and genuine humanity *may* be the possession of the so-called harlot. On the other hand, there are a number of books that give a very false and unwholesome representation of women prostitutes, books which would have us believe that a brothel is a leaden casket containing nothing but genuine pearls.

All this confusion in thought and action, where sexual ethics are concerned, only goes to prove that women, bewildered by centuries of sex-slavery, have been unable to lead the sexual emancipation with a firm purpose. Many of them have been overhasty in condemning the monogamous marriage, the evolutionary attainment of ages, and which, all its mistakes notwithstanding, invested the husband and father with solemn responsibilities. Too many have shown scant respect for the duty to faithfulness and sexual self-control, which, when everything is said, contributes great ethical values. In a word, women have not—to the extent hoped for thirty to forty years ago—shown themselves capable of a moral development, at once progressive and conservative. Earlier feminists firmly believed that love in its highest form would be secured by women's emancipation; they believed that women's self-support would eliminate all but love-marriages; that their equality with men in studies and work, in home and society, would bring about purer and higher morals, a more beautiful home-life, a more perfect motherhood. They little suspected, what has here been pointed out, that the self-support for many women has been so severe a task that marriage, on any condition, meant a deliverance; that women's purity and self-control, far from reforming men, frequently became a total loss; that the great love, for which the new women were to save themselves, often degraded into erotic adventures; that motherhood often is looked upon as an unwelcome interference in work or pleasure.

But even if the first apostles of feminism had suspected all this it would no more have silenced them than Jesus, had he been told that auto-da-fé and inquisition would follow Christianity. Because faith, among other things, signifies strength to endure the greatest of all disappointments—the shortcomings of the disciples. None of the worst disciples of woman-emancipation, not any of the errors brought about by the new morality, can nullify the truth that only woman's perfect equality with man in *education to work*, in *opportunity to work*, in *wages for work*, in *duty to work*, is the fundamental condition for final victory over sexual immorality, legal or illegal.

Every transition has brought in its train similar confusion of ideas and laxity in morals. Our race has never, in any province, reached the high morality born from within until the bands which upheld the morals imposed from without have first been loosened. At present we are living in a chaos where ancient and low instincts, in women as in men, fertilised with new and high ideas, have given birth to many monstrous forms of life. First, when these high new ideas have grown from thought to feeling and from feeling to instinct, the new morality will gather strength and stability. This morality is forcing its way in two hitherto quite diverging lines: *the individual's ethical right to self-assertion in love, and society's right to limit this self-assertion on behalf of the welfare of the race.* The first demand is based upon the growing insight into the immense differences between individuals in regard to the constitution of their souls in general and to their erotic needs in particular. The second demand follows the evolutionary birth of a new ethical principle—eugenics. This idea shows, by the swiftness with which it is gaining ground, that the morality which is organically bound up with life possesses a power of growth quite independent of established laws, customs, and creeds. The moral laws of eugenics sometimes cause one of those so-called "crimes" which suddenly reveal the existence of a new moral condition of mind. Such ethical "crimes" are repeated until they give rise to new conceptions of right and finally to new laws. A "crime" of this sort is committed by the mother who puts to death a child which is in every particular unfit for life. Another such "crime"—where the motive is individual egotism in compact with social altruism—is the deliberate motherhood of certain unmarried women. Working hard for their livelihood these women have afterwards supported their children and sometimes also the children's father when his inability or disinclination to work rendered him without means. Many earnest authors, for instance, Grant Allen in *The Woman who Did*, and the Dutch Cecilia de Jongbeck van Donk in her book *The Dawn*, have described a "crime" of this kind,—the *moral* motherhood of an unmarried woman; and at the same time they have shown the moral blindness of those who condemn such a one while they are glad to see their own and their friends' daughters make "good marriages" with degenerate but rich men. In many cases it is still considered a moral "crime" for a wife to dissolve a marriage which she feels to be degrading when there is no spiritual bond.

These divorces are deliberate indictments of the proprietorship that marriage yet is supposed to invest in man. Such divorced wives have often exchanged an economically splendid existence for a life of severe labour, all on account of their conscience.

Another ethical "crime" is "race suicide" in cases where the mother knows that the child would suffer degeneracy in consequence of the father's iniquities. Ethical may also be called women's revolt against the unreasonable waste of energy, personal and social, in bringing more children to life than may well be cared for.

Woman's new realisation of her human right to self-preservation, of her duty to cultivate her spiritual and physical energies and to use them also in her own interest, not alone in that of the race, is perfectly compatible, even when revealed in the "crimes" mentioned, with the new eugenic will: to produce a qualitatively better, not a quantitatively larger, new race.

That these new ethics sometimes make the actions of the most moral women similar to the actions of the most immoral ones ought at least not to excite those men and women who on the one hand advocate capital punishment for single murder, yet on the other hand glorify murder *en masse* in war! In the latter case, one is told that the motive determines ethics. But the very same people refuse to consider the motive in connection with women's above-mentioned "crimes."

During all these passionate conflicts about sexual morality, we are, on the whole, quietly and constantly advancing in regard to the elevating of future generations. A more rational care of children has already been introduced, a forward step demonstrable by the decrease of infant mortality. Further advance may be recognised in the fact that many women and men now break an engagement or a marriage when they find out that either party suffers from some hereditary disease. Increasingly numerous are the men and women who abstain from erotic relationship when they know themselves victims of such heredity. To be sure the great majority are still ignorant, or unscrupulous, in regard to the commands of eugenics. But public opinion is fast developing in this respect and is already beginning to influence conventions, which in turn will influence the laws. The demand of eugenics will finally become just as deep-rooted an instinct as the duty to defend the home country against outer foes, who, however, not even in the bloodiest battles, take as many lives or waste as many homes as do alcoholism, syphilis, tuberculosis, and mental diseases. A thoughtful modern person is tempted to agree with Spitteler, who presented a satirical description of a prize competition that resulted in the creation of the world. In this competition the laurel wreath was accorded to the artist who created a small perfect earth inhabited by only twelve supermen; which served as a suitable antithesis to the present bungle-globe, swarming with mortals.

Every person whose mind is not paralysed by the present nationalistic war colonisation and industrial politics, but who can still bend his thoughts toward culture, must recognise that the improvement of the race can only take place through a strict selection of the human material; hence the diminution in nativity need not in itself be a national evil symptom, but what is dangerous and immoral is that the worst element is allowed to multiply without restrictions while the women best fitted for motherhood are unable or unwilling to fill the high office; and finally that those of them who do become mothers are beginning to preach a "mother's sacrificial duty" not to bring up the children herself but to leave it to the community to train and educate them collectively. In later pages I shall return to this question which is for humanity so vital. Here I wish, only for the sake of completeness, to emphasise the fact that this at the same time is the most important of all woman questions. The answer to this question will determine whether women will continue to be the standard bearers of the morality they attained while upbuilding home and family, or if their morals will become more manlike in good, and also in evil, since every virtue that possesses substantiality also has its shadow. Only he who believes in "divine" moral laws can doubt that women's self-assertion must, on the whole, help to elevate humanity. But the very one who hopes this will likewise hope that the ancient womanly virtues—the motherly sacrificial spirit, and the wifely faithfulness, these virtues which were woman's before any one had dreamt of her independence—never shall rank among "outgrown" virtues, which a later age calls "weaknesses."

On the contrary, these virtues will be all the more needed when love is made the ethical norm for the relationship between men and women. Notwithstanding the countless individual differences which will appear more and more in these relationships, they are governed by a law as inflexible as the necessity for the presence of both oxygen and nitrogen in the air, namely, that love implies a "will to eternity" in the dual desire for faithfulness between husband and wife and for projected life in the new race. No emancipation must make women indifferent to sexual self-control and motherly devotion, from which some of the highest life values we possess on this earth have sprung. Let us remember that the best qualities of the sailor are still needed by the aviator, though the latter has a wider space in which to sail. Unless we realise this truth now we will learn it later by the number of victims sacrificed.

V

We are not helped to an understanding of the modern woman's moral uncertainty by the talk of the religious disbelief and the evil of the times. We face the results of the fact that women neither have been, nor are yet, fully liberated; the fact that for thousands of years they have learned to consider their value as sex beings as that by which they must buy all life enhancement whether noble or ignoble; the fact that sex has been the only sphere of woman's power, and that these circumstances have made her "over-sexed" as Charlotte Perkins Gilman rightly has pointed out. Hence it is unreasonable to speak of woman's morality in its present phase as of her new morals. Only a long enjoyed liberty will clearly show the social and psychological results of the efforts of the present age to equalise sex character, which, during the long period of woman's bondage, has been so differently developed in man and woman. First after some centuries of ethical and social culture on a par with man's, and of legal and economic equality, through a work which is so well paid that it does not exhaust either body or soul—first then will it be known whether women have developed a new "nature," or if the typical womanliness remains typical even of the daughters of the future. But in our calculations of probabilities we must not forget that within the next hundred years we shall witness another evolution which will have an enormous influence just

in regard to woman's prospective "nature."
I mean the transformation of our conceptions
of property and conditions of labour. There
is no more ethically promising aspect of
woman's liberation than the rôle it plays in
the great democratic revolution; that it coincides quite naturally with the increasingly
individualised socialism and the increasingly
socialised theory of evolution. Nowadays we
know that the "struggle for existence" is
counterbalanced by mutual helpfulness; that
the right of the stronger need not rob the weak
of his rights. Woman has good prospects
during her economic activity to escape demoralisation through unearned riches, unchecked
competition, unbridled enterprise. For all
this will gradually pass and simultaneously
the growth of women will experience self-
confidence that comes from economic independence and the consciousness of being
productive members of society. If we com-
pare the innumerable wives, who still do an
enormous daily labour in the homes without
receiving any other compensation than the
husband's gifts, with their self-supporting
sisters, we best realise the significance of
economic independence for morality. We

grasp how the whole woman sex will rise to an ethically higher plane through the independence that comes from well-paid work, when she need no longer use her cunning or her beauty to cajole the man into giving her what she needs for her development or her pleasure. To the extent that animals de luxe and beasts of burden in the shape of idle and worn-out women vanish, sexual morality will automatically rise above its worst blemish: the commercial value of the woman body.

But, some one asks, is the social morality really such, in a majority of women, that, having attained their full equality with man, legally, economically, socially, and politically, they are likely to deliberately collaborate in the social reconstruction? May not women in the classes which ought to be leading—because they possess the highest culture—show the same lack of social conscience as the men of the same classes? To be sure women are *now* showing great solidarity in the struggle for their rights. Women of all classes, labourers and duchesses, work together in the suffrage campaign and all national antipathies are bridged over by the common interest. And already this solidarity is in itself an ethical gain. But has it really penetrated deep enough into women's consciences, so that, when their own aims are won, it has power to overcome the class egoism which sustains the class struggle and the national egoism which maintains war? Moreover a victory is often followed by fatigue and apathy. Hence women's sacrifices, enthusiasm, and co-operation *during their struggle for equal rights* do not prove that women really have risen to a higher altruism, a wiser sympathy, a common fellow-feeling. The deciding evidence will be the *use women make of their new rights.* In this respect the present shows discouraging as well as hopeful signs.

The gravest danger is that so many of the best women do not realise the duties of motherhood, which are the most valuable to the race, to the nation, and to humanity at large. Hence it is all-important to regain on a higher plane the ethical synthesis of self-assertion and self-sacrifice which motherhood accomplishes already in earlier stages.

Ten years ago, in my book *Love and Marriage,* I presented a reform programme—further developed in the following essays—in opposition to collective upbringing of the children and work outside of the home for the mothers —the socialist and woman's-right platform common at the time.   In the meantime, the ideas of evolution and eugenics have emphasised the importance of the child; the sufferings of children have received more attention; it has become recognised that education is fraught with great responsibility and consequently there is need of thorough preparation in the educator.   I have recently noticed a socialist writer, of the capacity of Mr. Wells, point out that parentage "as a private enterprise, managed at the parents' own risk," must cease to exist.   As a curative, he offers the same solution that I do, and emphasises strongly that socialism disapproves both of the childless loose sexual relationship and of the patriarchal family rights.   Socialism wishes to institute a *free* marriage in which husband and wife, in every respect perfect equals, with social subsidies and responsibilities to society, will be well able to bring up the new generations.

For the time being, the conflicts may become sharper between subjective and objective morality; between the rights of the individual and the rights of society; between woman's demands for herself and the demands made upon her by the family. The easiest stage of woman emancipation will soon be a thing of the past, the stage of struggle for rights. Then follows the most difficult period of struggle for production; for simultaneous creation of men and works, or two creative impulses which cannot at the same time be wholly satisfied nor be entirely segregated to fill two different periods in a woman's life. Many women have become morally vacillating just because of this dilemma. Some have tried to get out of it by treating love and motherhood as incidentals. But, if the race is to rise ethically, women should not learn of men to take love and parental duty as an episode. On the contrary, man should learn of woman to consider it as a matter of vital importance. In this respect, we note encouraging signs of the times among young men, who in many respects have adopted a higher sex morality, probably because evolutionistic philosophy has entered more deeply into the minds of the young men, and probably also because the greater difficulty to win a woman's love has refined man's erotic emotions. It is a sad feature in the history of woman's morality that it is now often the woman who makes immodest advances to the man, and that when a child is the result the man is often more pleased than the woman. Obviously nothing will more certainly destroy what preceding generations have tried to build up in manly sex morality than that women themselves take this morality lightly.

Not until women look upon love and motherhood as holy powers of life, to be reverenced as solemn and sacred, shall the sexual morality of both sexes follow an ascending, not a descending curve. And whatever our philosophy of life otherwise may be, we must all confess ourselves believers in what a German thinker has called "Der Ascendismus," if life, and particularly moral life, is to have a meaning. Only by improving the quality of the human race in successive generations, through a more and more responsible, enlightened, and loving parentage, shall we attain a more beautiful future. No individual morality, be it that of men or women, is sufficient to raise the value of life, even if the world were delivered from capitalistic production, armed peace, and senseless war. All that the women now promise themselves and humanity of a new order of existence in which purity and responsibility shall characterise the relationship of the sexes, as love and justice the life of the peoples, will not materialise in the near future, even if all the women of the world are enfranchised. And naturally so, because the social and political work of the best women can no more succeed in changing the morality of the majority than the work of the best men has succeeded in so doing, neither will external transformations change the fact that the majority of women and men stand on a low plane physically, morally, and intellectually; hence improved social conditions cannot eliminate want and crime.

Yet all that we dream of the future may at last be realised, and realised through the women, if the mothers of the next thousand years will consider as their highest happiness the duty to promote in their children the evolution necessary to attain a higher humanity.

Motherhood, which is the fountainhead of altruistic ethics, and which has been woman's particular field for moral action, must consequently become the culmination of her functions as an ethically thinking, feeling, and acting being. But not merely in a direct sense. When women, in youth and early middle age, have fulfilled their, at that time, highest moral duty—to bear and rear the new race—and in this work have employed all the culture which their new rights enable them to acquire, then the time for spiritual motherhood has arrived and will occupy the latter part of their lives. Frederik van Eeden has well expressed the function of this motherhood in words something like these:

In the age when woman, according to the old theory, was worn out and done with, she may now possess a new and great mission: to increase the common fund of human knowledge by contributing her own stored treasures of intuitive wisdom.

It was woman's intuition which the ancients worshipped in the form of the Norne and the Sybil. It is this intuition which again must be respected and active in order that humanity may rise ethically and æsthetically as it has already risen materially, intellectually, and, especially, technically.

Men have gathered the materials for building a more beautiful and moral world—it can be built only by women and men working together.

II

Motherliness

Womanliness means only motherhood;
All love begins and ends there.
ROBERT BROWNING.

FIFTY years ago no one would have thought
    of writing about the nature of mother-
liness.   To sing of motherhood was then just
as natural for ecstatic souls as to sing of the
sun, the great source of energy from which we
all draw life; or to sing of the sea, the mysterious sea, whose depth none has fathomed.
Great and strong as the sun and the sea,
motherhood was called; just as tremendous
an elemental power, a natural force, as they—
alike manifest, alike inexhaustible. Every
one knew that there existed women without
motherly instincts, just as they knew of the
existence of polar regions on the globe; every
one knew that the female sex, as a whole, was
the bearer of a power which was as necessary
for life's duration as the sun and the sea, the
power not only to bear, but to nurture, to love
and rear and train. We knew that woman,
as a gift from Nature, possessed the warmth

7   97

which, from birth to death, made human life human; the gift which made the mother the child's providence, the wife the husband's happiness, the grandmother the comfort of all. A warmth which, though radiating most strongly to those gathered around the family hearth, also reached those outside the circle of her dearest, who have no homes of their own, and embraced even the strange bird as it paused on its journey. For motherliness was boundless; its very nature was to give, to sacrifice, to cherish, to be tender, even as it is the nature of the sun to warm, and of the sea to surge. Fruitfulness and motherhood received religious worship in the antique world, and no religious custom has withstood the changes of the times so long as this.

Many ideas have become antiquated and many values have been estimated afresh, while the significance of the mother has remained unchallenged. Until recently, the importance of her vocation was as universally recognised as in the days of Sparta and Rome. The ideas of the purpose for which she ought to educate her sons changed, but the belief in the importance of training by the mother remained. Through the Madonna Cult the

Catholic Church made motherhood the centre of religion. The Madonna became the symbol of the mother-heart's highest happiness and deepest woe, as embodied in the Virgin-Mother's holy devotion at the manger and the sacred grief of the Mater Dolorosa at the cross. The Madonna became the symbol of woman's highest calling, that of giving to humanity its saviours and heroes—those heroes of the spirit, so many of whom have borne witness to the importance of the intrinsic power of womanhood as a guide, not only to earthly life, but also to those metaphysical heights about which the greatest of them all has testified that: *Das Ewigweibliche zieht uns hinan.*

Das Ewigweibliche is nothing but the well of maternal tenderness, that power of love whereby woman's intuition takes a short cut to the heights which man's thought reaches by a more laborious path. Great poets have perceived that motherhood is not only the mighty race-renewer. Björnstjerne Björnson says that "all creating is of mother origin"; in other words, that all the qualities which the child craves of the mother, the work craves of its creator: the vision, the waiting, the hope, the pure will, the faith, and the love;

the power to suffer, the desire to sacrifice, the ecstasy of devotion. Thus, man also has his "motherliness," a compound of feelings corresponding to those with which the woman enriches the race, oftener than the work, but which in woman, as in man, constitutes the productive mental process without which neither new works nor new generations turn out well. Man's experience of the mother's influence on his life causes him—at least among the Romanic peoples—to include the mother in his worship of the Madonna. And whenever a man dreams of the great love, he sees a vision of motherly tenderness fused with the fire of passion.

In Art, that great undogmatised church, man has not wearied of interpreting that dream, of glorifying that vision in word and colour. Even the woman-child, with motherly action straining the doll to her breast, kindles his emotion; he would kneel to the maiden who, unseen, displays her tender solicitude for a child, to the "Sister" who brightens the sick-room, to the old nurse in whose face every wrinkle has been formed as a cranny of goodness. They all touch his emotion in revealing the loveliest of his possessions in mother or wife; if he has neither, then the things which he most yearns to have, and which he most warmly desires about him in his last hours. Whether the individual was doomed to yearn in vain or not, that motherliness existed has always been felt to be as certain as that the sun existed, even though the day be overcast. Humanity could, one thought, count on the warmth of motherliness, as for millions of years we may still rely on the warmth of the sun.

II

During those earlier periods, motherliness was but a mighty nature-force; beneficial, but violent as well; guiding, but also blind. As little as they discussed the question of the natural division of labour, which had arisen because the woman bore, nurtured, and reared the children, and—in literal as well as in spiritual sense—kept the fire on the hearth, even less did they doubt the natural "mother instinct" being sufficient for the human family. The instinct sufficed to propagate the race, and the question of not only propagating, but elevating, had not yet been thought upon.

Even such as it has been, motherliness has achieved enormous gains for progress. Although not yet consciously cultivated, it has been the greatest cultural power. Through research into the origin of humanity and into its early history, it became clear to us as previously explained that motherliness was the first germ of altruism, and that the sacrifices for their progeny which the higher animals, and even the lowest races of mankind, imposed upon themselves were the first expressions of the consciousness of kind, out of which later the social feeling gradually developed with its countless currents and unmeasurable deeps.

With the primitive peoples, who lived in a state of war of all against all, there was only one spot where battle did not rage, where the tender feeling, little by little, grew. Among the older people, mutual depredation was the established order; only the child craved help; and in helping the child, father and mother united. The child made the beginning of a higher relation between the parents. In the man, the fatherly duty of protection took the form of war and hunting, which developed the self-assertive, "egoistical" qualities; while the woman's duties developed the self-sacrificing, altruistic feelings.

Motherliness, which in the beginning was but the animal instinct for protecting the young, became helpfulness, compassion, glad sympathy, far-thinking tenderness, personal love—a relation in which the feeling of duty had come to possess the strength of instinct, one in which it was never asked *if*, but only *how*, the duty should be fulfilled. And though the manner of showing the feeling has undergone transition, the feeling itself, during all the ages that it has acted in human life, has developed until, in our day, it has grown far beyond the boundaries of home. The man's work is to *kindle* the fire on the hearth, the woman's is to *maintain* it; it is man's to *defend* the lives of those belonging to him; woman's, to *care* for them. This is the division of labour by which the race has reached its present stage.

Manliness and womanliness became synonymous with the different kinds of exercise of power belonging to each sex, in their separate functions of father and mother. That the mother, through her imagination dwelling on the unborn child, through her bond with the living child, through her incessant labors, joys, and hopes, has more swiftly and strongly developed her motherliness than the father his fatherliness, is psychologically self-evident. The modern psychologist knows that it is not the association of theory, but the association of feeling, which is the most important factor in the soul-life. But besides feeling, which belongs to the unconscious sphere, and which, like the roots of the plant, must remain in the dark soil that the tree may live, we have *will* to guide our thoughts. What is present in the soul, what directs our action, what spurs our effort, *that* is what we, with all our will, as well as feeling, hold dear. Thus there accumulated in the female sex an energy of motherliness, which has shown itself so mighty and boundless a power that we have come to claim it as a constant element and one not subject to change. And this energy grew so great because the hitherto universally conflicting elements in human life reached their oneness in mother-love; the soul and the senses, altruism and egoism, blended.

In every strong maternal feeling there is also a strong sensuous feeling of pleasure,— which an unwise mother gives vent to in the

violent caresses with which she fondles the
soft body of her baby—a pleasure which thrills
the mother with blissful emotion when she
puts the child to her breast; and at that same
moment motherliness attains its most sublime
spiritual state, sinks into the depths of eternity, which no ecstatic words—only tears—
can express. Self-sacrifice and self-realisation
come to harmony in mother-love. In a word,
then, the nature of motherliness is altruism
and egoism harmonised. This harmony makes
motherhood the most perfect human state;
that in which the individual happiness is a
constant giving, and constant giving is the
highest happiness. Björnson's words, "a
mother suffers from the moment she is a
mother," and the declaration of countless
women that they never realised the meaning
of bliss until they held the child to their breast,
are fully reconcilable in the nature of motherhood.

What torrents of life-force, of soul, tenderness, and goodness have flowed through
humanity from the motherliness of the true
mothers, and the mothers who have not borne
children. All the bodily pangs and labours
which motherhood and mother-care have cost

age after age, is the least of their giving. All the patient toiling which millions of mothers have imposed upon themselves when they alone have reared and fed their children, all the watchful nights, all the tired steps,—all that mothers have denied themselves for the sake of their children, is not the greatest of their sufferings. Their greatest sorrow is that expressed in the poem, written by a man, wherein the mother throws her heart at her son's feet. The son, as he angrily stumbles over it, hears it whisper, "Did you hurt yourself, my child?"

During the thousands of years that motherliness was of this sort, women had not yet been seized with the modern and legitimate desire, *sich auszuleben*, to drain the wine of life. The one desire of their souls was *sich einzuleben* to lose themselves in the lives of their dear ones in their own world, often narrow indeed, yet for them a world grown great and rich through the joy of motherhood in creating. The mother had labour and trouble no less than the working-woman of to-day, but then she was in the home. She could quiet the crying of the little child, take part for a moment in its play, give correction or help;

she was at hand to receive their confidences when the children came in with their joys or griefs. Thus she wove of little silken threads a daily-stronger-growing band of love, which, throughout all the changes of life, and wherever the children afterwards went into the world, held their hearts close to her own.

And when a mother, later, sat alone and yearned, how she lived in and through her children!

Though all were not like Goethe's mother,— Goethe, whom we could have loved even more if he had oftener visited his glorious mother,—yet she is typical of the many, many mothers in whom motherliness has been so strong that it has lived by its own strength, so great that it has developed all the powers of their beings. And these mothers became complete individualities of dignity and worth, although their life-interest was centred, not in a work of their own but in the child to whom they had given the best of themselves. They were mothers of whom great sons have testified that from them had they got their own essential qualities. Those mothers were not "characterless" beings, upon whom the women of our day, bent on the complete expression of their wonderful lives, look down. No, they were in the noblest sense liberated. Their personalities were enriched through wisdom and calm power. They were ripened into a sweetness and fulness through a motherliness which not only had tended the body, but which had been, in deepest meaning, a spiritual motherhood.

Besides these glorious revealers of motherliness, there has always been the great swarm of anxious bird-mothers, who could do no more than cover their young with their wings; great flocks of "goose-mothers," mothers who with good reason were called unnatural, just because it was never doubted that motherliness was the natural thing, something one had a right to expect—the wealth which could have no end.

III

Scientific investigation into the form through which, consciously or unconsciously, the power of motherliness was expressed in the laws and customs of the past, and further research into that compound of feelings and ideas which shaped and gave rise to the traditions of savage tribes, came simultaneously with the era of Woman-Emancipation. At the same time there took place a deep transformation in the view of life, during which all values were estimated anew, even the value of motherliness. And now the women themselves borrow their argument from science, when they try to prove that motherliness is only an attribute woman shares with the female animal, an attribute belonging to lower phases of development, whereas her full humanity embraces all the attributes, independent of sex, which she shares with man. Women now demand that woman, as man, first of all be judged by purely human qualities, and declare that every new effort to make woman's motherliness a determining factor for her nature or her calling, is a return to antiquated superstition.

When the Woman Movement began, in the middle of the last century, and many expressed fears that "womanliness" would suffer, such contentions were answered by saying that that would be as preposterous as that the warmth of the sun would give out. It was just in order that the motherliness should be able to penetrate all the spheres of life that woman's liberation was required.

And now? Now we see a condition of things alluded to in the first chapter, a constantly decreasing birth-rate on account of an increasing disinclination for motherhood, and this not alone among the child-worn drudges in home and industry, not alone among the lazy creatures of luxury. No, even women strong of body and worthy of motherhood choose either celibacy, or at most one child, often none. And not a few women are to be found eager advocates of children's upbringing from infancy outside of the home. Motherhood has, in other words, for many women ceased to be the sweet secret dream of the maiden, the glad hope of the wife, the deep regret of the ageing woman who has not had this yearning satisfied. Motherliness has diminished to such a degree that women use their intelligence in trying to prove not only that day-nurseries, kindergartens, and schools are necessary helps in case of need, but that they are *better* than the too devoted and confining motherliness of the home, where the child is "developed into a family-egoist, not into a social modern human being!"

IV

Some years ago, I wandered through the Engadine, the place where the two men who, for our day, have strongly emphasised the importance of motherliness found inspiration—Nietzsche, summer after summer, and Segantini, year after year. Segantini has often painted, not only the human mother, but also the animal mother. And he has done both with the simple greatness and tenderness of the old masters who, in the Madonna and the Child, glorified the wonderful mystery of mother-love. Segantini, who lived and died in the Alpine world where life is maintained under great difficulties, noted principally the importance of the mother-warmth during the mere physical struggle for existence. Nietzsche again, the lonely writer and seer of humanity's future, emphasised not only the significance of motherliness in a physical sense, but also in a sense hitherto barely perceived, *of consciously re-creating the race*. He knew that the instinct first of all must be developed in the direction of sexual selection, so as to promote the growth of superior inborn traits. He knew also that women needed to be educated to a perfected motherliness, that they, instead of bungling this work as they are apt to do to-day, may come to practise the profession of motherhood as a great and difficult art.

This new conception is ignored by those who advocate community-upbringing instead of home-rearing, because most mothers, among other reasons, are *to-day* incapable as educators, and because parents *to-day* often make homes into hells for children. What hells institutions can be, seems to be forgotten! Almost every child is happier in an ordinary, average home than in an admirable institution, because every child needs—has needed, and will continue to need—a mother's care; but we must see to it that this care will become increasingly efficient. And what a strange superstition, that the *teachers* of the future will all be excellent, but—that the *parents* will remain incorrigible.

As yet have we even tried to educate women and men to be mothers and fathers? This, the most important of all social duties, we are still allowed to discharge without preparation and almost without responsibility. When the words of Nietzsche, "A time will

come when men will think of nothing except
education," have become a reality, then we
shall understand that no cost is too great when
it comes to preserving real homes for the
purpose of this new education. And there is
nothing which in a higher degree utilises all
the powers of womanhood (not alone those of
motherliness) than the exercise of them in the
true, not yet tried, education of the new
generation.

All women, even as now all men, must learn
a trade whereby they can earn their livelihood,
—in case they do not become mothers, as well
as before they so become, and after the years
of their children's minority; but during those
years they must give themselves wholly to the
vocation of motherhood. But for most women it ought still to be the dream of happiness,
some time in their lives, to have fulfilled the
mission of motherhood, and during that time
to have been freed from outside work in which
they only in exceptional cases would be likely
to find the same full outlet for their creative
desire, for feeling, thought, imagination, as
is to be found in the educative activity in the
home. But so unmotherly are many women of this age, that this view is considered

8

old-fashioned and (with the usual confusion of definitions) *consequently* impossible for the future.

When already they say the women of to-day want to be "freed" from the inferior duties of mother and housewife, in order to devote themselves to higher callings, as self-supporting and independent members of society, how much more will that be the case with the women of the future! As these "higher callings," however, for the majority consist, and will continue to consist, in monotonous labour in factory, store, office, and such occupations, it is difficult to conceive how these tasks can possibly bring greater freedom and happiness than the broad usefulness in a home, where woman is sovereign—yea, under the inspiration of motherhood, creator—in her sphere, and where she is directly working for her own dear ones. Neither can it be understood how the care of one's own children can be felt as a more wearisome and inferior task than, for instance, the laborious work of a sick-nurse, or school teacher, who, year in and year out, works for persons with whom only in exceptional cases she comes in heart-contact.

If women meanwhile continue to look upon the work of mothers and house-mothers as in itself burdensome and lowering, then, naturally, the care of children and of the home will gradually be taken over by groups of women who, on account of their motherliness, choose to occupy themselves with children and household duties.

If this "freedom" is the ideal of the future, then, indeed, my view of motherliness, as indispensable for humanity, is reactionary; but it is reactionary in the same way that medicine reacts against disease. And has our race ever been afflicted by a more dangerous disease than the one which at present rages among women: the sick yearning to be "freed" from the most essential attribute of their sex? In motherliness, the most indispensable human qualities have their root.

Women who summon all their intelligence and keenness in their endeavour to prove that motherliness is *not* the *quinta essentia* of womanhood verily need a Minerva Medica, as portrayed in the Vatican relief, the goddess of wisdom with the symbol of the art of healing! And she will surely come when the time most needs her.

The phrase, "the course of progress tends to the dissolution of the home," shows how little we understand the words we use. Progress implies also dissolution, decay, retrogression, and death. In the progress of a disease attacking culture, a new renaissance must come, if not for the people, then for the truths, which though temporarily dimmed will be seen in a new light by new peoples. From time to time has this been the case with the emotions of patriotism, of religion, and of liberty. No fundamental values, indispensable to humanity, are lost; they return reinforced. Motherliness has not been lost even in those who show a lack of it in their personal lives. They have converted it into general service. When women at last have become fully emancipated, then the enormous sums of energy which now are invested in agitation will be set free: to be used partly for social transformation, partly to flow back with fresher and fuller power into the home.

Very likely there will always be a number of unmotherly, of sexless, but useful working ants. Women geniuses, with their inevitably exceptional position, may increase. Possibly also the type of *hetaira* frequent in our day—

women who devote themselves to a career which makes them independent of marriage. They wish to be lovers, but lovers who captivate not alone by beauty, but also by intellectual sympathy. That these women do not want the care of children, when they do not even want motherhood, is but natural.

In that future of which I dream, there shall be neither *men* who are ill-paid and harassed family supporters, nor wives who are unrewarded and worn-out family slaves. Then all home arrangements shall be as perfectly adjusted as they are now the reverse, and all home duties be transformed by new ways of work, which shall be lighter, cheaper, quicker. Thus, woman will actually be "freed" in respect to those burdens of the home-life from which she ought to and may be freed, freed so as to be spared the necessity of giving over the care of her children to nurseries and kindergartens, where even the most excellent teacher becomes mediocre when her motherliness must embrace dozens of tender souls.

If, on the other hand, "progress" takes the road leading toward the breaking up of the home,—the ideal of the future for the maternal, —then the future state will be a state of herd-people. But the more our laws, our habits of work, and our feelings become socialised, the more ought education itself in home and school to become *individualised*, to counteract the danger of getting fewer personalities while institutions increase. And individual upbringing can be carried on only in homes where mothers have preserved the nature-power of motherliness and given this power a conscious culture.

V

The supposition that motherliness has its surest guide in its instinct is therefore a superstition which must be conquered. In order to be developed, motherliness must exist in one's nature. The matter must be there so as to be shaped; this is obvious. But the feeling in itself may, like all other natural forces, work for good or for evil; the feeling itself often shows, even in motherliness, the need of the evolution in humanity which the poet foreshadows, when we at last shall see "the ape and tiger die."

As motherliness has been sung more than it has been understood, we have lived in the illusion not only that it was inexhaustible, but that its instinct was infallible,—that for this sacred feeling nature had done everything and no culture was needed. Hence motherliness has remained until this day uneducated. The truth that no one can be educated *to* motherliness—any more than a moon can be made into a sun—has been confounded with the delusion that the mother-instinct is all-sufficient in itself. Hence it has often remained blind, crude, violent; and "instinct" has not hindered mothers from murdering their children by ignorance, and from robbing them of their most precious mental and physical possessions.

This sentimental view of motherliness as the ever holy, ever infallible power, must be abandoned; and even this province of nature brought under the sway of culture. Motherliness is as yet but a glorious stuff awaiting its shaping artist. Child-bearing, rearing, and training must become such that they correspond to Nietzsche's vision of a race which would not be *fortgepflanzt* only, but *hinaufgepflanzt*.

Motherliness must be cultivated by the acquisition of the principles of heredity, of race-hygiene, child-hygiene, child-psychology. Motherliness must revolt against giving the race too few, too many, or degenerate children. Motherliness must exact all the legal rights without which woman cannot, in the fullest sense of the word, be either child-mother or social-mother. Motherliness thus developed will rescue mothers not only from olden-time superstition, but also from present-day excitement. It will teach them to create the peace and beauty in the home which are requisite for the happy unfolding of childhood, and this without closing the doors of the home on the thoughts and demands of modern times. Motherliness will teach the mother how to remain at the same time Madonna, the mother with her own child close in her arms, and Caritas, as pictured in art: the mother who at her full breast has room also for the lips of the orphaned child.

Many are the women in our day who no longer believe that God became man. More and more are coming to embrace the deeper religious thought, the thought that has given wings to man created of dust, the thought that men shall one day become gods! But not through new social systems, not through new conquests of nature, not through new institutions of learning. The only way to reach this state is to become ever more *human*, through an increasingly wise and beautiful love of ourselves and our neighbours, and by a more and more perfect care of the budding personalities. Therefore, if we stop to think, it is criminal folly to put up as the ideal of woman's activity, the superficial, instead of the more tender and intimate tasks of society. How can we hope for power of growth when the source of warmth has been shut off?

The fact that the thought of our age is shallow in regard to this its most profound question—the importance of motherliness for the race—does, however, by no means prove that the future will be just as superficial. The future will probably smile at the whole woman-question as one smiles at a question on which one has long since received a clear and radiant answer! This answer will be the *truly free* woman of the future, she who will have attained so fully developed a humanity that she cannot even dream of a desire to be "liberated" from the foremost essential quality of her womanhood—motherliness.

III

Education for Motherhood

I

"A time will come when men will think of nothing except education."

NIETZSCHE.

THE optimism with reference to the mothers of the future which I have expressed in the foregoing is based on my habit of counting by epochs in judging the probable future of humanity. The optimist is often right. But only if he can wait—some hundred years!

The modern woman's view of motherhood, as I have endeavoured to show in the first essay, is not calculated to nourish optimism. This view is the natural result of the spirit of the age which is determined fundamentally by the two great vital forces, physical and spiritual, which, since the morning of the race, have had decisive influence on its destinies,— economics and religion. During the last century, economic conditions have been regarded as of greater importance, and religion of less. The souls of nations, as well as the individual soul, have been earth-bound in the fullest sense of the word. Investigations of earth and nature and the utilisation of all resources have occupied a race which has made the spirit of Aladdin's lamp a slave of utility; which, with greedy heart, has gained the whole world, but in the meantime has heedlessly forfeited its own soul.

Science and desire for gain have marvellously broadened the sphere of man's power over an external world. Simultaneously with this the emancipation of woman has proceeded. The world invaded by woman, both needing and demanding work, has not been a world in which holy voices have spoken of high things. It has been a world in which strong and hot hands have grasped what to their age seemed the kingdom of heaven: material wealth which gave its possessors the power, the honour, and the glory. Gain has been God, and man this God's prophet. Work has been divine worship, especially such work as produced riches. The possibilities of satisfying steadily increasing cravings for pleasure, and of living an ever more care-free and secure life, have multiplied. And women did not stem the tide; they followed it.

In logical conjunction with the raising of utility as the highest of life-values, a highly gifted American woman has offered her programme for the solution of the conflicts between woman's labour and motherhood, namely, the rearing and educating of children outside the home. Successive institutions are suggested for the bottle-period, kindergarten, and school-age, and so on. Thus, she contends, will the parents, who are usually poor educators, be supplanted by trained and "born" educators; the children would stand in visiting relations to the individual home with its too warm and emasculating tenderness, while in the institutions they would get the bracing air and the training for social life demanded in this age, instead of the egotistical attitude of family life. The social activities of the mothers of the well-to-do classes and the outside work of the wage-earning mothers make mother-care only a figure of speech, and the children are neglected. But, on the other hand, by this plan of reform, the bodies as well as the souls of the children would be well cared for by specialists. The mothers

could calmly devote themselves to their gain-
ful work and their social duties. The child's
need of the mother and the mother's need of
the child is a prejudice which must vanish
with all other superstitions from lower stages
of culture, if the mothers are to be coequal
with men, community members, capable of
work, and if the children are to be well reared
for the social vocations which must soon
determine the trend of all lives.

This view of Charlotte Stetson (now Mrs.
Gilman) coincides somewhat with that of the
great African author, Olive Schreiner. Both
these writers emphasise rightly the fact that
since woman's home work no longer has the
same productive value that it had in an age
when she was the one to prepare the raw
materials and to produce all the necessities
for the household, the women of the leisure
class, under the shibboleth "the care of the
home," have become the largest class of social
parasites of contemporary times, who pay
with their body for the freedom from work
that the men gain for them. Women have
become "over-sexed" because to enhance
their sexual attraction has been the surest
means of obtaining an idle life through

matrimony. Until this and similar economic interests vanish from marriage, love
cannot be pure nor can the position of the
wife be one of true human dignity. Long
ago, in the eighteen-thirties, these truths
were expressed by the great Swedish writer,
C. J. L. Almqvist.[1]

If the Spartan plan above mentioned were
really a solution of the problem, there would
be no occasion for further talk about general
education for motherhood. In that case, all
young girls could go straight on toward professional training with a remunerative vocation
as their goal. And this would be not only a
personal, but a national economic gain. For
the personal energies and the money spent in
acquiring a profession would not be wasted,
as is now so often the case, if motherhood were

[1] C. J. L. Almqvist fled from Sweden in 1851 and went to
New York in the fall of the same year, there calling himself
Professor Gustavi. He supported himself by teaching languages
and acting as reporter on newspapers; he travelled extensively,
visiting Upper Canada, Niagara, St. Louis; lived in Belleville,
in Chicago, and Philadelphia, and was in St. Louis at the time of
the Civil War. Enthusiastic Unionist and admirer of Lincoln,
he hastened to Tejas in Mexico, lost some manuscripts in Tejas,
and with difficulty reached Washington, where he met Lincoln.
He returned to Europe in 1865. In case any one in America
should happen to remember anything about him, communication
thereof would be most gratefully received.—THE AUTHOR.

but a short interruption in a woman's professional work.

This programme, outlined but briefly since it is well known in the United States as in Europe, has the enormous advantage of making clear the dilemma before which many women who work for their livelihood play ostrich, namely, that a woman cannot be a competent outside worker, working from eight to ten or more hours a day, and at the same time a housewife and mother who performs well the duties these vocations demand. That which many women with exceedingly small claims upon them still insist on—that they are well able to manage outside work, housekeeping, and the rearing of children simultaneously—is just what the reform-programme refutes, making it plain that the present attempts at compromise have resulted in a lessening of value together with an enormous overstrain.

I, too, am convinced that the present state of affairs is untenable from the economic, hygienic, ethic, and æsthetic point of view. A radical transformation is needed. But I hope that this will go in an opposite direction from the one indicated above.

The programme for the abolition of home-training rests on three unproved and un-demonstrable assumptions: first, that women's mental and spiritual work in the home—the creating of the home atmosphere, the management of the housekeeping and the upbringing of children—is of no "productive" value; secondly, that parents are incapable of acquiring proficiency as educators unless they are "born" educators; thirdly, that nature amply provides such "born" educators, so that the many thousands of institutions—with a professional mother for about every twenty children—could be supplied with them in sufficient quantity and of excellent quality.

These assumptions emanate from a comparison between the present untrained mothers and trained educators, and between all the dark sides of the home and the light sides of collective upbringing. But on so warped a comparison we certainly cannot base a demand for the discontinuance of the upbringing in the home.

II

The past gives us proof enough that woman's creation, the home, has been her great cultural contribution to civilisation. And even the present main trend of the desires and feelings of the race shows that the home has not lost its value. But nothing is more certain than that there has awakened a need within the people for a renaissance of the home. In my opinion, such a renaissance can come only through a new marriage, where the perfect equality and liberty of both husband and wife are established; through a strict responsibility towards society in regard to parentage outside as well as within marriage; through education for motherhood; and, lastly, through rendering motherhood economically secure, recognising it as a public work to be rewarded and controlled by society.

Thus the problem seems to me more complex, involving greater expense, and therefore more difficult of solution.

And yet, it must be solved. The socially pernicious, racially wasteful, and soul-withering consequences of the working of mothers outside the home must cease. And this can only come to pass, either through the programme of institutional upbringing, *or* through the intimated renaissance of the home. The self-supporting women of the

present day do not want again to become
dependent solely upon the husbands' main-
tenance in order to be able to fulfil the duties
of a mother in the home.   And thus there remains only institutional upbringing *or* motherhood regarded as a social work.

During the child's first seven years, years
that determine its whole life, its educator
cannot well fulfil her mission without having
a daily opportunity to observe the child's
nature, in order by consistent action to influence it, encouraging certain tendencies and
restraining others.   This alone precludes the
mother's working outside the home.   To an
even greater degree must her work outside
the home be rejected in favour of that most
essential education,—the indirect,—which ra-
diates from the mother's own personality,
from the spirit she creates in the home.   Like
the direct education, the indirect cannot be
accomplished in stray moments snatched from
professional work.   A home atmosphere is not
a condition which stays permanent of itself,
one of those works of art which once created
remain unchanged.   The creating of a home is,
on the contrary, a kind of art which has this
in common with all art of life—that it de-

mands the artist's continuous presence in body and soul. A home life where the mother's unceasing contribution of self is lacking is like a drama on a film.

Wherever the great and beautiful work of art, a home, has come into being, the wife and mother has had her paramount existence in that home though her interests and activities have not necessarily been limited to its sphere. But husband and children have been able to count on her in the home as they could count on the fire on the hearth, the cool shade under the tree, the water in the well, the bread in the sacrament. Thus upon husband and children is bestowed the experience which a great poet gained from his mother. "All became to her a wreath!" A wreath where every day's toil and holiday's joy, hours of labour and moments of rest, were leaf and blossom and ribbon.

The wise educator is never one who is "educating" from morning to night. She is one who, unconsciously to the children, brings to them the chief sustenance and creates the supreme conditions for their growth. Primarily she is the one who, through the serenity and wisdom of her own nature, is dew and sunshine to growing souls. She is one who understands how to demand in just measure, and to give at the right moment. She is one whose desire is law, whose smile is reward, whose disapproval is punishment, whose caress is benediction.

Sometimes fathers, too, are endowed with this genius for education. And it would not be the least of the consequences of outside upbringing if the children were to lose not only the daily influence of the mothers but also that of the fathers. Because the fathers are the breadwinners, and also because of their lack of training for fatherhood, this influence is as a rule insignificant. But it is very important that this state of affairs be changed. According to the testimony of an American author,[1] the increasing predominance of women teachers in America is already cause for anxiety, and with good reason, for the good order of things in school, in the home, in the community, demands that men and women co-operate as equals, having like authority and like responsibility. But since a division of labour on the whole is unavoidable, this division must be determined by the experience

[1] Earl Barnes, in *Woman in Modern Society.*—THE AUTHOR.

that in the labour market, in the majority of cases, men are just as able as women, and often better able, to perform the work women perform.

In the home, on the other hand, men cannot supplant the spirit and activities of women. Neither can the contribution of the wives and mothers to the homes be replaced by that of professional women within or outside the homes. Can the heart in an organism be replaced by a pumping engine, however ingenious? Any reform programme which does not consider these realities falls under the wise judgment of the shrewd Catherine II.: "Reforms are easily accomplished on the patient paper. But in reality they are written on the human flesh, which is sensitive." Especially is this true of the child who, moreover, must submit to the influence of his educators, unable to choose or evade them. The author of the programme means that the mothers who are gifted as educators should bring up about twenty other children, together with their own. But each young soul needs to be enveloped in its own mother's tenderness, just as surely as the human embryo needed the mother's womb to grow in and the baby the mother's breast to be nourished by. According to the programme referred to, each child would be allotted a twentieth part of motherliness; the mother's own children would receive no more than the others.

Of the real outcome of this plan a prominent American woman gave me a touching illustration. As sole support of her son, she had been compelled to send him to a boarding-school where many little motherless boys were brought up. When she went to visit her boy, the other boys fought with him for a place on her lap, so hungry were they for a moment's sensation of motherly affection!

That many children are unhappy in their homes does not prove that the same children would be happier in an institution; only of such children as were transferred from bad homes to good institutions could this be hoped. That many a careful home education has failed does not prove that the children brought up in a particular home would have turned out better in an institution. The very best institution cannot show the consideration for a child's individuality, or furnish the peace and freedom for the development of a talent, that an average middle-class home can.[1]   The more individual a child is, the more it suffers by the uniformity and the levelling forces which are imposed upon it already by the day school.   And how much more must this be the case in a boarding school!

On the other hand, we have the manifold testimonies given by great personalities of the boundless influence of a mother's, of a father's, understanding affection, in the development of the child's individuality.   In the children's resemblance to the parents, the latter have a guide to the understanding of the children's inherent qualities, which the teachers lack.   And if, on the one hand, these resemblances contain the seeds of conflict, on the other, they furnish various possibilities of influence.

[1] The excellent French writer, Rosny (*aîné*), in *Le Fardeau de la Vie* touchingly describes the sufferings a child experiences in always having witnesses to everything: his rest and his play, his tears and his joys; of never having a corner to himself; of ever being surrounded by cries, laughter, noise, and jokes; of never having an hour's perfect peace or liberty; of always feeling every emotion of the soul and every action observed, every occupation subjected to interruption.

The children of the poor experience similar sufferings in their homes, a condition which can be remedied only by better housing conditions.   Similarly, it would only be institutions furnishing a separate room for each child which, in some degree, might alleviate the torture described by the French writer.—THE AUTHOR.

As against all the cases where the tyranny of the parents—now increasingly rare—has forced the children into an erroneous walk of life, may be put those where the parents have discovered their children's talents and have encouraged them in the right direction. Sometimes a good teacher has done the same. But a teacher, with some tens of children, has not the same opportunity to observe the individual child as have the parents. The mistakes of the teacher are, therefore, far more numerous than those of the parents. If these children would, in many cases, have chosen other parents, they would, in most cases, have chosen other teachers.

"Born educators" with keys to the children's souls in their pockets are, indeed, the unredeemable promissory notes of the institutional programme. The assurance that the children in collective institutions would be cared for only by "born educators" is as untenable as would be a promise that their musical training would be directed by nobody short of a Beethoven! "Born educators" are not only as rare as other geniuses, but are also most difficult to discover. For how can they demonstrate their genius except in the practice of educational work? And often they find no opportunity to educate; an examination can, for instance, just as little reveal their soul power as it can that of a poet. The brilliant and eloquent graduate often is, and will continue to be, victorious in competition with the "born educator." And, as everybody knows, the result frequently is that the greatest abominations occur at institutions where perverse principals infernally torment the children—principals chosen by boards of trustees who have felt convinced of having made the best choice! But even in those cases where the choice has been good, how much remains to be desired!

One pedagogue, for instance, may have excellent ideas, but be lacking in nobility of character. Another may possess great psychological insight, but no ability in the psychologically correct treatment of children. Here may be found pedagogical genius, but without warmth of heart. There, heart but no sagacity. Another is of a despotic nature, and in spite of all pretty talk of children's rights, he violates them to make the little ones conform to his ideas. Still another is vacillating and has no authority.

And if thus already the first-rate teachers are deficient, how much more so will this be the case with those mediocre teachers of whom every school and boarding-school has a majority!

These professional educators,—as they are called in the programme for upbringing outside of the home,—so far from being wholly filled by their calling, spiritually liberated from all side interests, which, according to the same programme, are supposed to impede the parents' capabilities as educators,—these professionals are very much like other people, absorbed by their own sympathies and antipathies, conflicts and rivalries, in which the children frequently become involved.

The parents would stand in the same relation to all these institutions as they now do to the day schools, in that what they objected to they could seldom change. But if the parents were not content to remain simply automata, who deliver the child-material to the institutions, they must, on the one hand, endeavour to assert their own opinion as against the institutions which cause contentions, and, on the other, try to make use of the children's home visits for counteracting such influence of the school as they consider unfavourable. But here they would meet with the same fundamental difficulty which arises in cases where children, as a consequence of divorce, are periodically with either father or mother. So many requisites for understanding are lacking: constraint and strangeness have to be overcome; a nervous tenderness or a cold criticism often destroys attempts at intimacy. In a word, even the best institutions would show the same dark sides as do the homes, or similar ones, but unaccompanied by the bright sides of the homes, which outweigh their shortcomings.

Let us assume, however, that the choice of principal in one of these proposed institutions has been a happy one. Yet such a teacher has not the spontaneous love for the child which may, to be sure, on the one hand, cause parental blindness, but, on the other hand, gives the clearness of vision which belongs to love alone. At best the teacher extends to the children a general love, or a personal love to one child here and there. But it is just this personal love which the human soul needs in order to burst into blossom.

The conditions here indicated furnish one

of the reasons why children from charitable institutions hardly ever become prominent members of society. The main reason, it is true, is that the children for whom society has had to care in institutions have often sprung from poorly equipped parents. Moreover, to be sure, the prominent individuals in a nation are always few in comparison with the others. Still, if we can expect one great genius in each million of inhabitants, one in a million institutional children may be expected to be really excellent. But has a single one ever appeared? Is not, on the contrary, the insignificance of such children a rule with few exceptions? And must not this partly depend on this very system of upbringing?[1]

Even where the child-material is excellent, as for example in the English country schools for boys, observations have led to the belief that these schools are more favourable for the preservation of the national type—for good as well as evil—than for the development of the individual. Here, as in other boarding-schools, certain social virtues are developed, certain

[1] In America this question has been answered in the affirmative by some investigator, who at the same time came to the conclusion that the "Cottage" system gives better results in every way than the large institutions.—THE AUTHOR.

qualities useful in public life. But the springing up of new types, stronger individual aptitudes, more sensitive and fine soul life is not favoured by any kind of collective education extending through the larger part of youth. A period of institutional life has often been a splendid thing for children who have been lonely or spoiled at home, has hardened them, forced them to subordinate their own egotism, taught them consideration for others, and common responsibilities. But even if institutions can thus rough-plane the material that is to become a member of society, nevertheless they cannot—if they take in the major part of the child's education— accomplish that which is needed first of all if we are to lift ourselves to a higher spiritual plane in an economically just society: they cannot deepen the emotional life. Continuity of impressions is a first condition for such a deepening. But the upbringing outside of the home, which would leave the nursing infants in Miss A.'s hands, the kindergarten children to Miss B., the primary school children to Miss C., the higher grades to various Misses, would again and again disrupt the fine fibres with which the child-heart has become tied to these various mother-substitutes. At last the heart would lose its power of attachment, just as is the case when children spend their lives travelling and only get into hotel relations, never into home or homeland relations with the world.

The psychological progress of the development of the emotions indicates that the child should learn to love a few in the home and in its native place; that the soul should broaden to feelings for the comrade circle, finally to embrace society and humanity. Every effort to change the order in this progress of growth is as fruitless as to put plants in the ground blossom downward and roots in the air. Want of insight into those spiritual conditions of growth is the principal error in the programme or collective upbringing. What youth would have left of soul after such an education would barely be sufficient for social and community purposes; for the needs of the personality it would not suffice.

And even if collective education, when the school age is reached, were arranged as it is in some of the German (in many ways excellent) *Landerziehungsheime*,[1] where a small

---

[1] These schools were founded by Dr. Herrmann Lietz after the pattern of Abbotsholme in England. His schools are: Ilsenburg

number of children and teachers live in a separate cottage and constitute the so-called "family," in the long run it would be only a poor substitute for the natural family, where care and anxiety, help and comfort, memories and hopes, work and festivity crystallise around a nucleus, combine and intensify the emotions, while in a larger, often-changing circle even the most beautiful impressions become weakened and shallow.

The very worst suggestion which has appeared from any side is that of the family colony, with common kitchen and dining-room, common play-room and care of the babies, et cetera. Even this would give the mothers freedom to pursue professional work and yet in some measure retain the home for the children. But if Satan announced a prize competition for the best means of increasing hatred on earth, this reform proposition ought to receive the first prize. That seclusion and introspection which are necessary for mutual communication between husband and wife,

---

for small boys, Haubinda for the intermediary grades, and for the high-school period Bieberstein. Paul Schub's *Landerziehungsheim Odenwaldschule* has provided for the home feeling and the individual development to the greatest extent possible in a boarding school.—THE AUTHOR.

if they want to grow into complementary personalities, would be as difficult to attain as silence in the market-place for the enjoyment of music. The unfortunate children growing up in such a family colony would be cross-questioned, commissioned, corrected, and teased. Such a colony, far from broadening the children's interests outside their own circle—as the proposers contend—and teaching them amiable social ways, would cause torment to independent spirits, and increase dulness in the constrained. Besides, children seldom have more affection to spend than they abundantly need for their parents, and parents seldom have more patience than they abundantly need for their own children.

Countless causes for friction would arise among the grown-ups as a result of differences between the children, between husbands on account of wives, and between wives on account of husbands. Though in the beginning all were harmony, it would end in discord, after the well-known pattern of most similar or even less intimate groupings.

These reasons against the disintegration of the home might be multiplied. I wish now only to emphasise one point of view, which I have often advanced before. Women have always, and not least in America,[1] by the trend their own social work has taken, been able to show to what an extent society needs that the specially womanly, that is, motherly, feelings and outlook be asserted in action. These motherly ways of feeling and thinking have acquired their characteristics and their stability by reason of the hitherto existing division of labour, in which the task of making the home and rearing the children created "womanliness" with its strength and its weakness, just as the outward struggle for existence, the competitive field of labour, created the strength and weakness of "manliness."

That women, during their protected, inwardly concentrated life, would acquire other emotional standards, other habits of thought than men, is obvious. Hitherto, however, they have had very small opportunities to invest their stored wealth in the upbuilding of this "man-made world." Consequently, there is a crying need of womanliness, especially motherliness, in public life. But motherliness

[1] I have received valuable information in this respect through Rheta Child Dorr's book, *What Eight Million Women Want.* — THE AUTHOR.

is no more permanent than any other state of the soul. Soul sources are like the water in nature, sometimes abundant, sometimes scant, clear to-day, turbid to-morrow, now flowing, then again frozen—all according to the soil through which it finds its way, and the temperature it meets. If now the division of labour be changed to such an extent that all women during the whole work-period—that is, about forty years—devote themselves to outside occupations, while a minority of women, who are often not mothers themselves, professionally fill the need for child-rearing, then motherliness will diminish generation after generation. For it is not alone the bearing of children, neither is it the upbringing alone, that develops motherliness, but both together are needed. The result will be that women's contribution to society will be similar to that of men. They will fill with stones the "springs in the valley of sorrow" which the homes, in spite of everything, have been hitherto in our hard and arid existence. The new world, which the women soon will have a hand in making, will be no more beautiful, no warmer, than the present. Even a very much more rational and just social order cannot furnish compensation for all the subtle and immeasurable riches which directly and indirectly have flowed from the home.

If the destruction of the homes were the price the race must pay for woman's attainment of full human dignity and citizenship, then the price would be too high. If the female parasites cannot be gotten rid of in any other way than by driving all women out of the homes to outside departments of labour, let us rather, then, allow the parasites to flourish, since of two social evils this would be the lesser.

But humanity will not have to choose between two such evils. The parasitical family woman just as much as the worn-out family drudge, the family egoism piling up wealth and the economically harassed family life, as well as other ignoble constituents which riches as well as poverty bring into the homes, are all part and parcel of the present social order. A society which sharply restricts inheritances, but protects the right of all children to the full development of their powers; which demands labour of all its members, but allows its women to choose between the vocation of motherhood or outside work; a society in which attempts to live without work will be dealt with in the same manner as forgery—such a society is coming. In this society, mother-care will be a well-paid public service to which an effectual supervision is given, and for which state control is accepted. Without such radical social transformations, renaissance of the family life is not even conceivable. And it is not likely to become actual before the changing orders of economics and a new religion combine their forces.

III

As I have already stated, economy and religion determine the trend of life, especially that of family life. And for this reason the tide of the age, which has already turned women outward, is likely to wax stronger until a new religion once again shall kindle the soul of the people with a burning desire for great spiritual values.

Certain signs have appeared, indicating that the religious as well as the economic transformation is in progress. The heartbeat of humanity has always gone thus: after the outflowing, the inflowing—from the surface back to the heart. The new religion will probably not be a "refined" Christianity. But the deepest experiences of the race, to which Christianity gave expression in myths and symbols now worn out, will reassert themselves in a new form. And the highest ideas which Christianity has given to humanity will again become life-determining forces, although on other grounds.

The crisis through which all the assets generally considered "Christian" and "feminine" are now passing arose out of their sharp contrast to the present social development or outlook on life. Women have no longer that Christian faith, as a mainstay against the power of the times, which among other things made them willing to accept as many children as it "pleased God to send." Implicit devotion and self-sacrifice are no longer women's ideal. The legitimate individualism which has made the modern women determined also "to live their own lives" has, with many, resulted in a decision to throw off "sexual slavery in the family." From this individualism women can be converted only through a new religious belief, namely, that every human being "lives his own life" in the greatest and most beautiful sense when his will is in harmony with that mighty will to create of which the whole evolution—of culture as well as of nature—bears witness.

But the will to create, which is the mysterious innermost nature of life, nowhere reveals itself more simply or more strongly than in that love out of which new beings spring, and in the parental devotion to these new beings. From the point of view of the new religion, the professional and social work, which by many modern women is considered an obstacle to motherhood and of greater social value than the latter, will only be a "tithe of mint and anise and cummin" when husbands and wives, well equipped for parenthood, do not give the race their flesh and blood. All that the intelligence and genius of men and women can do for eugenics and the care of infants, for education and schools, is of small consequence so long as it is lavished on a human material constantly shrinking in value because produced by physically and psychically inferior parents, while those who have the making of good parents cannot afford, or have not the will, to supply children to the race. Or, as a famous botanist has vigorously expressed it: "A single microscopic cell from which one great human being springs is of greater importance to the race than the painstaking efforts of a hundred thousand childrearers and educators with a child-material below par."

This conception must become dominant before any "education for motherhood" can be effective. Thoughts and emotions, will and imagination, must be converted and sanctified through a religion that considers the present superficial culture as a fall of man. The low ideal of happiness held by an irreligious race—a more and more luxurious, easy, gliding, automobile existence—will lose its attraction for humanity through the religious awakening. Men and women will once more dream of noble and dangerous deeds. We will have an epoch of aviation also in a spiritual sense. The heroic attitude toward and in life, which the world of antiquity and Nietzsche in the modern world represent, will again become the ideal of happiness which guides the leaders of the race. Even the many will again desire the deep feeling, the strong emotions and difficult tasks,—despite the dangers, sufferings, and sorrows they may bring. For the ideal of happiness will not then, as now, be the easiest existence, but the one which allows the greatest expenditure of power.

For the majority of women family life offers this more toilsome and troubled, but also more rich and joyous existence. But not family life alone! Power expands also in taking part in the organisation of a more and more perfect society, in a more concerted progress toward a wiser and higher moral goal. This too is a collaboration with the Will to create, an adjusting of one's own individuality to individual assets beyond, or, in other words, a form of the new religious worship.

The morning star which augurs the birth of the new religion is already visible on the horizon. Not only economic and democratic forces are at work for the new social order; there are also religious ones. To the same extent that these forces increase in strength we shall draw nearer to that state which is to relieve the present chaotic and energy-wasting society, the present soulless and aimless existence.

And not until then are we likely to have mothers well trained for the vocation of motherhood and well cared for by society during the discharge of this duty.

A new time comes, as a rule, with quiet and small steps, only rarely with great, swift strides. One small step is the training of girls and boys in sexual hygiene and in their duties toward themselves as future parents. Another is the realisation that by a better physical development through gymnastics, athletics, dancing, etc.—a development highly important for the new race—strength and beauty will be gained also for the children. A third is the recognition in Europe, as well as in America, of the obvious need of a training for the inherently womanly vocations. To begin with, we have discovered that it is only an empty phrase to assert that industry has wholly supplanted the business of the household, since very many tasks remain which have to be done in the home. And further, we have grown to understand that to purchase all the necessities of life ready-made lowers the family's standard of living and increases the cost more than if the wife performed certain work in the home. We have begun to see that the value of the wife's industrial work does not, from a national economic point of view, compensate for the family's higher cost of living, the women's indisposition toward motherhood, and incapacity for it, the neglect of the children and the home and the consequent increase of alcoholism and criminality, and finally the constantly growing expense to the state of the rearing and care of the children in public and charitable institutions.

As a result of these observations, women especially, but also men, have begun to advocate cooking-schools, courses in domestic science and household economics. Such courses are given in conjunction with the public schools and colleges, or as independent courses, whether or not combined with the care of children. "Mother schools," child-training schools, kindergarten schools, lecture courses in child-psychology and in experimental psychology, everywhere are springing into existence. In a word, efforts are being made to remedy the ignorance of the young women of the present generation as to the mission of the home—an ignorance which is the result, on the one hand, of the early entering into industrial labour, on the other hand, of the long studies.

We are ready to deplore the colossal mismanagement which has gone on century after century in allowing women to come unprepared to their most important vocation,—for society and for the race,—the bearing and rearing of children. Information as to sexual matters is still, by many, considered an abomination—in Germany a girl was expelled from a boarding-school because she possessed a scientific book on the "sex-life of plants"!—but it is now everywhere imparted by all thoughtful educators. The moderate feminists, at least in Europe, are using all these measures in their endeavour to make women professionally capable in their old department of labour. They understand that only increased capability can give the inwardly directed expenditure of woman's power a new dignity, make it a new social asset.

Considering this training by itself, I believe that the cooking course has its right place in the early teens when it is enjoyed by most girls as a change from book-studies, and as a knowledge of which they may easily make use. But I do not believe that that age is the psychologically correct time for the more serious and important education in the art of home-making and the duties of motherhood.

The fundamental evil of the present school-system is its tendency to line up the manifold desirable teachings for the young like soldiers on parade, namely, on graduation day. This is an insurmountable obstacle to thoroughness and veracity in instruction, qualities which cannot be fully attained without perfect peace for both teachers and pupils—a peace which is never associated with fixed courses and examinations. Without serenity, no knowledge can fully ring out, vibrating through thought, feeling, will, and imagination. But only by such a resonance does the knowledge manifest itself as living, only thus does it become a power for growth within the individual.

And this is what education for motherhood must accomplish; otherwise it is a failure. During the early "teens" the young girls' minds are already crammed with abstract knowledge which frequently they have neither desired nor needed. Then comes this education for motherhood for which they have no direct use, and it comes at a time when their minds are mostly filled with thoughts and dreams about the unknown life which attracts all their yearning, though as yet in indefinite forms. It consequently follows that they will come absent-minded to the instruction in the vocation of motherhood, and when later in life they stand before the reality, they will have forgotten most of this teaching, as they forget so much of the other instruction they have received without longing for it, and without the personal assimilation referred to above.

Even if one takes this instruction as seriously as, for example, the German woman suffragists desire,—who endeavour to introduce an obligatory year-long course for all girls, as a preparation for motherhood,—such preparation, for the reasons mentioned heretofore, would in reality be far from as effective as a training given some years later. In my opinion, girls as well as boys, after having at about the age of fifteen finished the common preparatory school—which ought to be entirely free from examinations—should devote themselves to their special professional training, which, in the case of the majority, would be completed at about the age of twenty. And this is the age at which I would advocate a year of social service for women as well as for men. In the states that enforce military training, such a period of service is already required of the men and it often lasts several years. I consider a parallel service for women the right education for the care of home and children. And this period of training should be set at the psychologically well adapted age when many of the young women already look forward to a home of their own, or at least have become conscious of a longing for home and children.

The year of training should be divided into three courses:—

1. A theoretic course in national economics, the fundamental hygienic and æsthetic principles for the planning of a home and the running of a household. This course would hardly need to include practical exercises, since sewing and cooking classes, and the like, form a part of the curriculum in the present-day schools, and thus the first principles of domestic science are there imparted.

2. A theoretic course in hygiene, psychology, and education for normal children, with directions for the recognition of abnormalities.

3. A theoretic course in the physical and

psychical duties of a mother before and after the birth of a child, and the fundamental principles of eugenics.

To these theoretic courses must be added practical training in the care of children, which should embrace knowledge of the child's proper nourishment, clothing, and sleep; its physical exercise, play, and other occupations; and its care in case of sickness and accident. Children's asylums, day-nurseries and hospitals, and mother-homes (where mothers with children would find refuge for shorter or longer periods) would give opportunity for such training led by the teachers.

Already in the year 1900 (in *The Century of the Child*, first edition), I had proposed a service for women similar to the compulsory military service for men. Such propositions had been made in Sweden even earlier from several quarters. But they had only referred to the obligatory training of women in the care of the sick and their compulsory service as nurses in time of war. My plan, on the other hand, was that the training should principally comprise domestic science and the care of children, although the rudiments of hygiene and therapeutics ought also to be considered.

In 1900, no one took up my proposition, not even in order to attack it. During the last twelve years, this same proposition, but quite independently of me, has been put forth from many sides, not alone from Sweden, but from Norway, Germany, and elsewhere, and by men as well as women. Some of these—rather unfortunately in my opinion—have connected the question of such a year of social service for woman with the question of woman suffrage. This has come from quarters where it is considered that men's right to suffrage answers to their military duty. For my part, I have never connected these two questions, since I consider that the duty of paying taxes, equal for men and women, corresponds to their equal rights of suffrage, and, besides, that society's need of the women's point of view as well as of that of men fully justifies their eligibility to office. And, if we seek a parallel to man's sacrifice of life and limb or health on the battlefield, we find it in child-bearing, a battlefield where many women give their lives or become invalids for the rest of their days.

The duty of training for social service as mother or soldier, in my opinion, naturally follows from the education that society has given the young, an education which, in regard to professional training, they must repay by efficient work in their various professions, but also by preparing themselves to defend and promote the culture of which they are beneficiaries. The natural division of labour will then be that the men prepare themselves to defend the country in case of an impending peril, and to be helpful in times of disaster, while the women prepare themselves to defend and care for the new generation on which the future depends.

In the distant future, when military service shall no longer be needed, and at present, in countries where it is not enforced, all young men ought to have some such training as that of which the Scout movement is, in a certain sense, a beginning—a training in readiness and ability to assist in case of natural calamities and other accidents which may befall society or individuals. Even now, it is the soldiers and seamen who, at times of fire, railroad and mine accidents, floods and earthquakes, show themselves the best helpers, because of their habits of discipline, and of swift and efficient action. Boys ought to be taught—as is done here and there already—the preparation of the plainest dishes and the simplest mending of clothes, in order that they may not be utterly helpless in any situation in which they may find themselves in life. And the young man should, during his year of social service, receive instruction in the first principles of eugenics and hygiene.

Young men and women ought also, as a matter of course, to get some knowledge of the essential features of the structure of society. This may be given already during the school period—as has very successfully been tried at an excellent coeducational reform school in Sweden—if the knowledge be not imparted through dry discourses. In this school, the young people are allowed, under the guidance of an expert teacher, to play at parliament two hours a week during some years. They have elections, committee-meetings, party divisions, motions, and discussions, just as in the national legislature. Even the rudiments of national economy can in such a manner be made living and interesting.

That all of this directly belongs to woman's education for social motherhood, and indirectly also to her vocation as the mother of future members of society, needs no further proof. For men, as well as for women, the social-service year would not be wasted even if many would have no occasion personally to use for their own individual benefit all the knowledge gained. There exists no woman who does not, in some way or other, come into contact with children. And it is increasingly rare for women not to find opportunities in social work to use the knowledge gained during a year's instruction in the care of children, hygiene, eugenics, domestic science, and national economy. But far beyond and above the benefits which understanding of this or that individual case would bring, is the awakening to social responsibility and the levelling of class distinction which such a year of obligatory social service would bring to the daughter of the millionaire and the factory girl alike.

As guides in the instruction of young women I would choose noble matrons, serene as priestesses, who themselves have fulfilled the mission of motherhood—women ripened into sweetness of wisdom, and with power to impart vividly the fruits of their experience to the young who, some day standing before the serious task of making a home and bringing up children, may perhaps by a single word of advice remembered in time save life's happiness for themselves.

As a transition toward a legally established social-service year for women, I think it might be a good plan to make a course in housekeeping and the care of children a condition of the right to marry. This would result in the private establishment of such courses everywhere. But, on the one hand, the state would have no control over their character, and on the other, these courses would mostly be taken during the above-mentioned and least appropriate age, while in cases when this would not be true, they might come as an unwelcome compulsion later on. In consideration of all these reasons, it is best to fix our eyes upon an obligatory year of service for women as a goal to be realised in the near future. The nation which tried this out would find its health and prosperity increased after a few generations in a measure that would thoroughly compensate for the cost involved. Such a cost need not, however, be as great as it is for the compulsory military training of men. To be sure, certain buildings would have to be erected,— suitable homes for the teachers and students who were not living in the neighbourhood of the training centres,— but appropriate lecture-halls would, in most cases, already be found on the spot. And while the service of the men does not confer any direct benefit to society in times of peace, the service of the women would place a large working force at the disposal of society for the care of the sick and of children and of all in need. In each centre, various energy-saving combinations would be possible. As an example may be mentioned that in Stockholm the feeding of poor children has been combined with the schools of domestic science. These embrace not only cooking and similar subjects, but also a course in the care of children, which in turn is combined with day-nurseries. Dining-rooms for working-women are also combined with the cooking-school. By wise, womanly organisation, there are consequently not less than six socially useful enterprises which directly support each other.

These suggestions suffice to show in what direction one must go in order to make practicable the use of the year of social service for women. Different conditions in different nations, and in various districts within each country, would dictate a variety of applications and a detailed programme would be as impossible as unnecessary.

Only certain essential conditions would need to be established everywhere. In the first place, a higher marriage age for women, the making of the legal marriage age for women the same as for men, twenty-one, has been proved to be conducive to the betterment of society and the race. Secondly, that the year between twenty and twenty-one be established as the year for social service, although—as is now the case for men—an earlier or later entering into service for valid reasons might be allowed. Thirdly, that complete freedom from service must be granted for reasons similar to those which now exempt men from military service.

In analogy with men, the women under obligation to serve ought to have free choice, within certain limits, in regard to the place of training, and also in regard to the selection of the practical and theoretic courses in which they would participate. For example, it would be foolish to waste time on such courses as have already been taken during medical or normal-school studies, and so forth. And, similarly, it would be a great waste of energy if one already graduated a trained nurse were commanded to do duty a hospital, or if a capable and well-inform child-nurse were sent to a children's home, d so on. The object should be so to arrange t training that each one to the greatest possib xtent would fill up the gaps in her knowledge.

After some generations of such ear education, it would be found that, just as th training for the teacher's calling has supplied the countries with good teaching forces, while the same forces untrained would have remained insignificant; the education for motherhood would supply the various nations with many good mothers well able to fulfil the duties of the home. Such "born educators" as did not become mothers would find work enough in institutions where children must be cared for by society because of the death or the viciousness or the work of their parents.

The attitude of the women, once they have gained full suffrage, toward the questions herein dealt with, will be the great test of the nature of their social motherliness. If they comprehend that the education of the mothers, and the rendering secure the functions of the mothers, is the life-question of the race, they will then succeed in finding the means of meeting these demands.

This sounds too optimistic to many readers. But did humanity ever halt helplessly before any of its vital needs?   Least of all could this happen in America, where the very air reverberates with songs of faith in the power of will, with the hope of realisation of most wonderful dreams.   From the Pilgrim Fathers, from the wars of independence and secession, we have strong evidence of the power of will over the destiny of the American people. Ever since, in my youth, I listened to Emerson's prophetic words, and Whitman's songs of the creative power of the soul and of the pliability of life in the moulding grasp of this power, I have again and again received new impressions—through thinkers, moralists, and sects—of this typically American spirit.   To be sure, it may sometimes lapse into boastfulness, or degenerate into superstition, as, for instance, when it is believed that the will can conquer every disease and even abolish death. But in itself this sovereign assurance of the victory of will, faith, and hope is the world's greatest power for overcoming evil with good.